Liquid Gold - The Global Crisis of Water

Sophia Fairview

Published by Independent Artists Network, 2024.

LIQUID GOLD - THE GLOBAL CRISIS OF WATER

First edition. February 29, 2024.

ISBN: 979-8224070664

Written by Sophia Fairview.

Table of Contents

Introduction

In a world where the tap's twist can summon water as if by magic, it's easy to forget that this clear, tasteless liquid is more precious than the finest wines of Bordeaux or the rarest whiskeys of Scotland. Imagine, if you will, a planet where water, not oil, commands the geopolitical stage, where nations rise and fall not on the whims of black gold but on the accessibility of clear, life-giving H2O. This is not the plot of a dystopian novel; this is the reality we are inching towards, a world where water is the true liquid gold.

As we embark on this journey through the pages of "Liquid Gold - The Global Crisis of Water," we find ourselves at the intersection of abundance and scarcity, a dichotomy as perplexing as it is critical. On one side, there are places where water flows with such abandon that it's used to sculpt lawns into emerald carpets in the midst of deserts. On the other, there are parched lands where a child's knowledge of water is as limited as their access to it, where the liquid is so scarce that it's a gift more precious than the most extravagant toy.

This dichotomy presents us with a stark reality: water, the very essence of life, the soul of our planet's ecological system, is becoming increasingly scarce. It's a crisis that unfolds in slow motion, a creeping catastrophe that, unlike the sudden devastation of an earthquake or hurricane, doesn't always command the immediate attention it demands.

But why, you might ask, is water so crucial? Beyond the obvious necessity for drinking, water plays a pivotal role in every aspect of our lives. It's the unseen protagonist in the story of civilization, the backstage hero that powers industries, nourishes agriculture, and shapes the very landscapes we call home. Yet, as indispensable as it is, we are depleting and polluting our water supplies faster than nature can replenish them.

This book aims to peel back the layers of the global water crisis, to explore not just the stark statistics that alarm and overwhelm, but to understand the human stories behind these numbers. It's a tale of paradoxes, of rivers running dry while elsewhere water floods and destroys. It's a narrative that requires us to question not just how we use water, but how we value it.

As we delve deeper into the complexities of the water crisis, we'll encounter the ingenious ways communities around the world are tackling water scarcity, from fog nets in the Atacama Desert to the revival of ancient qanat systems in Iran. These stories are testaments to human ingenuity and resilience, a reminder that while the situation may be dire, it is not devoid of hope.

So, let us embark on this journey with open eyes and curious minds, ready to laugh at the absurdities, marvel at the wonders, and confront the challenges of our relationship with water. After all, the future of "liquid gold" is not just a matter of environmental concern; it's a reflection of our values, our priorities, and our collective ability to change the course of history.

•

The Watershed Moment

In the annals of human history, water has been both the sculptor of landscapes and the ink with which our stories are written. From the cradle of civilization nestled by the banks of the Tigris and Euphrates to the mighty empires that rose along the Nile, Ganges, and Yellow rivers, water has been the lifeblood of society. It's a testament to its vital role that our ancestors chose to lay down their roots near water sources, intuiting that proximity to water meant not just survival, but the ability to thrive.

The narrative of humanity's relationship with water is as much about ingenuity as it is about reverence. Ancient civilizations not only worshipped water in its myriad forms but also engineered sophisticated systems to harness its power. The Romans built aqueducts, marvels of engineering, to quench the thirst of their sprawling empire. The stepwells of India, architectural wonders in their own right, were not just sources of water but communal gathering spots, illustrating the social dimension of water.

However, as the wheels of time turned towards the Industrial Revolution, our bond with water began to strain. The revolution brought with it unprecedented advancements and, with them, an insatiable thirst for water. Factories mushroomed along riverbanks, drawing copiously from this once-sacred resource, while spewing back a cocktail of pollutants. Rivers that had sustained generations became conduits of waste, their waters turning from life-giving to life-threatening.

This era marked a significant pivot in the human-water relationship, from one of symbiosis to domination. The advent of mechanized pumps and the construction of vast networks of canals and dams emboldened humanity's control over water, allowing for the expansion of agriculture into arid regions and the growth of cities in places water was scarce. Yet, this control came at a cost. Aquifers began to deplete, rivers to shrink, and lakes to vanish.

The rise of global populations and the relentless march of urbanization have only intensified the demand on water resources. Cities, with their concrete landscapes and dense populations, face the Herculean task of sourcing water for millions. The story of cities like Cape Town, which teetered on the edge of "Day Zero," a day when the taps would run dry, serves as a stark reminder of the fragility of our urban lifelines.

Moreover, the global narrative of water is one of stark inequalities. While some regions grapple with the excesses of water, facing floods and hurricanes exacerbated by climate change, others suffer from its absence. The disparity in water access across the globe lays bare the paradox of water: it is both abundant and scarce, a giver of life and a harbinger of hardship.

As we stand at this watershed moment, the need for a paradigm shift in our relationship with water is clear. The solutions of the past, grounded in control and consumption, are ill-suited for the challenges of the future. Instead, we must turn towards sustainability and stewardship, recognizing that water is not merely a resource to be exploited but a vital commons that must be protected and shared.

- The chapters that follow will delve into the innovative solutions and urgent actions required to navigate the complexities of the global water crisis. From the revival of ancient water conservation practices to the cutting-edge technologies of today, we will explore how humanity can reconcile its thirst for water with the imperative of sustainability. This journey is not just about securing water for future generations; it's about redefining our very relationship with the planet's most precious resource.

Rivers of Commerce, Oceans of Profit

Introduction

In the tapestry of global commerce, water has undergone a profound metamorphosis. Once revered as a communal treasure, essential for the sustenance of life and community, water has been steadily transmuted into a commodity, traded on markets and scrutinized for profit margins. This transformation marks a pivotal shift in humanity's relationship with one of its most fundamental resources, heralding a new era where the value of water is increasingly measured in currency rather than in its capacity to sustain life.

The commodification of water refers to the process by which water is treated as a marketable good, subject to the laws of supply and demand, rather than a basic human right. This shift has profound implications for societies worldwide, affecting everything from access to water, the quality of water available to the general populace, and the governance of water resources. As water becomes a commodity, the principles of equity, sustainability, and communal stewardship are often sidelined, giving way to a paradigm where water is a privilege rather than a shared necessity.

Section 1: The Commodification of Water

Historical Context

The journey of water commodification is not a phenomenon born of the modern era but has roots stretching back through history. In ancient times, water was a localized resource, managed by communities through a complex web of social norms and practices designed to ensure equitable distribution. However, as societies evolved, so too did the management of water. The Roman Empire, for instance, demonstrated early forms of water commodification through its aqueducts and baths, showcasing the ability to control and distribute water as a symbol of power and civilization.

The true acceleration of water commodification, however, aligns with the rise of global capitalism. The Industrial Revolution marked a turning point, where water became not just a necessity for life but a critical component of industrial processes. Rivers and lakes were harnessed to power factories, and waterways became conduits for the transportation of goods. This period laid the groundwork for viewing water as an asset, leading to the establishment of water rights that could be bought, sold, and traded.

Economic Forces

The economic forces driving the commodification of water are multifaceted, rooted in the interplay between scarcity, demand, and the push for privatization. Scarcity plays a pivotal role; as the availability of clean, accessible water diminishes due to factors like pollution, climate change, and overuse, its value as a commodity increases. This scarcity is not uniformly distributed, with certain regions facing acute water shortages while others remain relatively unaffected, creating a global market where water can be a tool for economic leverage.

Demand for water, driven by population growth, urbanization, and industrialization, further exacerbates the push towards commodification. As cities expand and industries grow, the need for reliable water sources intensifies, placing pressure on existing supplies and infrastructure. This demand has opened the door for privatization as a solution, championed by proponents as a means to increase efficiency, attract investment, and improve water distribution networks.

The global push for privatization has been facilitated by international financial institutions and multinational corporations, which advocate for the management of water resources by the private sector. This model posits that market-driven mechanisms are better suited to addressing the challenges of water scarcity and distribution. However, this approach has sparked significant debate and controversy, raising questions about the implications for access, affordability, and the right to water.

- The commodification of water, driven by economic forces and the global push for privatization, represents a fundamental shift in how water is perceived and managed. This transformation has significant implications for societies worldwide, challenging traditional notions of water as a communal resource and raising critical questions about the future of water governance, equity, and sustainability. As we delve deeper into the complexities of water commodification, it becomes clear that the stakes are not merely economic but touch on the very essence of life and the rights of people around the globe.

The Role of International Financial Institutions in Promoting Water Privatization

The global water crisis represents one of the most pressing challenges of the 21st century, characterized by a dire scarcity of accessible, clean water for billions of people worldwide. This crisis is exacerbated by a complex interplay of factors, including climate change, population growth, and unsustainable water management practices. In response to this growing crisis, there has been an increasing push towards the privatization of water resources as a proposed solution. This approach has been heavily influenced and promoted by key international financial institutions (IFIs), notably the International Monetary Fund (IMF) and the World Bank. These institutions have played a pivotal role in shaping global water management policies, advocating for privatization as a means to achieve efficient, sustainable water distribution and infrastructure development. This chapter examines how IFIs have utilized financial mechanisms and advisory roles to steer water privatization policies, fundamentally altering the landscape of global water governance.

Historical Context and Policy Evolution

The IMF and World Bank: Founding Purposes and Evolution

LIQUID GOLD - THE GLOBAL CRISIS OF WATER

The International Monetary Fund and the World Bank were established in the mid-20th century, primarily in response to the economic turmoil that followed World War II. Initially, their mandates were focused on stabilizing global economies and reconstructing war-torn nations. However, as the global economic landscape evolved, so too did the roles of these institutions. By the latter half of the 20th century, both the IMF and the World Bank had begun to play increasingly influential roles in the economic policies of developing countries, including those related to natural resources and, by extension, water management.

Shift Towards Privatization and Deregulation

The late 20th century witnessed a significant shift in global economic policies, with a growing emphasis on privatization and deregulation. This shift was driven by a belief in the superiority of market mechanisms over state-run systems in delivering services more efficiently and fostering economic growth. The IMF and World Bank were instrumental in promoting this shift, advocating for structural adjustment programs (SAPs) in developing countries. These programs often included conditions that required the privatization of state-owned enterprises, including those responsible for water management and distribution.

Promotion of Water Privatization by IFIs

The push for water privatization gained momentum in the 1990s, with the IMF and World Bank at the forefront of this movement. Key policy documents and statements from these institutions during this period explicitly promoted privatization as a strategic approach to water sector reform. The World Bank, for instance, argued that private sector participation could bring much-needed investment, efficiency, and innovation to the water sector, which was often plagued by underfunding and mismanagement in many developing countries.

One of the most influential documents in this regard was the World Bank's 1993 report, "Water Resources Management," which advocated for a comprehensive reform of water policies, including the encouragement of private sector involvement in water and sanitation services. This report marked a significant departure from traditional approaches to water management, positioning privatization as a key component of water sector reform.

The IMF, though less directly involved in water management policies, also played a crucial role through its financial support and structural adjustment conditions. These conditions often paved the way for privatization by requiring recipient countries to reduce public spending and deregulate their economies, indirectly promoting private sector involvement in water services as part of broader economic reform efforts.

Examination of Key Policy Documents and Statements

The advocacy for water privatization by the IMF and World Bank is evident in a range of policy documents and public statements. Beyond the 1993 World Bank report, subsequent publications and guidelines have consistently emphasized the benefits of privatization and public-private partnerships (PPPs) in the water sector. For example, the World Bank's "Private Participation in Infrastructure Database" tracks and promotes PPP projects in water and other sectors, highlighting the institution's ongoing commitment to privatization as a strategy for infrastructure development.

Similarly, the IMF's advisory papers and loan conditionalities for developing countries have frequently included recommendations for economic liberalization and privatization. While these recommendations are typically framed within the broader context of economic reform, they have significant implications for water management policies, often encouraging governments to open up their water sectors to private investment and management.

Financial Mechanisms and Conditionalities

The influence of International Financial Institutions (IFIs) on global water management policies extends significantly through their financial mechanisms. These mechanisms, including loans, grants, and debt relief programs, are often accompanied by a set of conditionalities aimed at restructuring the recipient countries' economic and policy landscapes. In the context of water management, these conditionalities frequently mandate reforms that pave the way for privatization, tariff increases, and the introduction of market-based principles into the sector. This section delves into the specifics of these financial mechanisms, explores case studies of their application, and discusses the rationale behind the push for privatization and related reforms.

Financial Mechanisms Used by IFIs

1. **Loans and Grants:** Loans and grants from IFIs like the World Bank and the IMF come with strings attached. These conditions often include structural adjustments in the economy, deregulation of various sectors, and specific reforms in water management practices. While loans provide the necessary capital for infrastructure development, grants are typically aimed at capacity building and technical assistance. However, both are leveraged to induce policy changes.

2. **Debt Relief Programs:** Debt relief initiatives, such as the Heavily Indebted Poor Countries (HIPC) Initiative, offer another avenue through which IFIs influence water sector policies. Relief is contingent upon the implementation of a range of economic reforms, including those affecting the water sector. These programs are often criticized for using debt relief as leverage to enforce privatization and other market-friendly policies.

Case Studies

Bolivia: The Cochabamba Water War

The Cochabamba Water War of the late 1990s and early 2000s in Bolivia stands as a seminal event in the global discourse on water privatization, vividly illustrating the potential consequences of International Financial Institutions' (IFIs) influence over domestic water policies. This episode not only underscores the social and political risks associated with the privatization of essential services but also serves as a cautionary tale about the importance of stakeholder engagement and the implementation of protective safeguards.

Background and IFI Influence

In the late 1990s, Bolivia was under significant pressure from international financial institutions, including the World Bank, to privatize its public utilities. This push for privatization was part of a broader neoliberal agenda promoted by IFIs, which argued that private sector involvement would lead to increased efficiency, improved infrastructure, and better service delivery. For Bolivia, a country grappling with economic difficulties, the adoption of these policies was also seen as a pathway to securing much-needed financial support and debt relief.

The World Bank made the privatization of Cochabamba's municipal water supply a conditionality of its loan agreements. This stipulation was based on the belief that privatization would help attract investment, improve water distribution, and reduce losses in the system. As a result, the Bolivian government passed Law 2029, which allowed for the privatization of the city's water utility.

The Concession and Its Aftermath

The concession for Cochabamba's water utility was granted to Aguas del Tunari, a consortium led by the multinational company Bechtel. Almost immediately, the company increased water tariffs by an average of over 35%, with some reports indicating that increases were as high as 200% for certain segments of the population. These rate hikes were catastrophic for many residents of Cochabamba, where the average income was among the lowest in South America. The increased tariffs meant that many families were spending a significant portion of their income on water, leading to widespread outrage and accusations that the privatization deal was negotiated without proper public consultation or transparency.

The Water War

The response to the tariff increases was swift and severe. A broad coalition of labor unions, rural workers, and community groups, led by a newly formed organization called the Coordinadora in Defense of Water and Life, initiated a series of protests, road blockades, and general strikes. These protests rapidly escalated into what became known as the Cochabamba Water War.

The government's attempt to quell the unrest through military force only fueled the anger of the protestors, leading to violent clashes. The situation reached a critical point when a 17-year-old boy was killed by military forces, galvanizing even greater opposition to the water privatization scheme.

Resolution and Repercussions

The intensity of the protests and the national and international attention they garnered eventually forced the Bolivian government to cancel the contract with Aguas del Tunari and repeal Law 2029. Water management was returned to a community-led utility, and the rates were reduced. However, the conflict left a lasting mark on Bolivia and became a symbol of the struggle against neoliberal policies and the privatization of natural resources.

The Cochabamba Water War also had significant global repercussions. It brought international attention to the issues surrounding water privatization and became a rallying point for anti-privatization activists worldwide. Moreover, it prompted a reevaluation of the role of IFIs in promoting privatization policies, highlighting the need for greater accountability, transparency, and public participation in decisions affecting essential services.

Tanzania: The Complexities of IFI-Driven Privatization

Tanzania's foray into water sector reform, particularly the privatization of Dar es Salaam's water utility in the early 2000s, offers a nuanced view of the challenges and pitfalls associated with International Financial Institutions' (IFIs) advocacy for privatization. Supported by the World Bank, the initiative aimed to enhance the efficiency, reliability, and accessibility of water services in Tanzania's largest city. However, the endeavor encountered significant hurdles, from contractual disputes to investment deficiencies and public dissent, ultimately highlighting the complexities of reconciling privatization efforts with public welfare and the intricacies of local governance.

Background and World Bank Involvement

The privatization of Dar es Salaam's water utility was part of a broader trend of economic reforms in Tanzania, encouraged by IFIs like the World Bank. These reforms were predicated on the belief that private sector participation could bring about much-needed efficiency and investment in the struggling public sector, including water services. In the late 1990s and early 2000s, the World Bank played a pivotal role in this process, providing financial support and technical advice for the privatization initiative.

The World Bank's support for privatization in Tanzania was aligned with its global agenda to promote private sector involvement in public utilities. The institution argued that such involvement would lead to improved service delivery and infrastructure development, crucial for economic growth and poverty reduction. In Dar es Salaam, the goal was to address the city's chronic water shortages, poor water quality, and inadequate infrastructure through privatization.

Implementation Challenges

The privatization process led to the awarding of a 10-year lease contract to City Water Services Ltd, a consortium involving a British water company, a German investment company, and a local Tanzanian firm. However, the initiative soon faced significant challenges:

1. **Contract Management Issues:** Disputes arose over the terms of the contract and the responsibilities of the involved parties. The Tanzanian government and the private consortium clashed over tariff rates,

investment commitments, and service targets, leading to a fraught relationship that undermined the project's goals.

2. **Investment Shortfalls:** One of the primary rationales for privatization was the attraction of private investment to upgrade and expand the water infrastructure. However, the expected capital investment from the private sector did not materialize as anticipated. The consortium faced difficulties in mobilizing the necessary funds, partly due to the lower-than-expected revenues and the challenging operating environment.

3. **Public Opposition:** The privatization of Dar es Salaam's water utility was met with significant public resistance. Critics argued that the move would lead to higher water tariffs, making access to clean water unaffordable for many of the city's residents. There were also concerns about accountability and the prioritization of profit over public service. The lack of transparency in the privatization process and the perceived sidelining of community stakeholders fueled distrust and opposition.

Outcomes and Reassessment

The privatization initiative in Dar es Salaam ultimately fell short of its objectives. In 2005, just a few years into the contract, the Tanzanian government terminated the agreement with City Water Services Ltd, citing the consortium's failure to meet the agreed-upon service and investment targets. The project's collapse prompted a reassessment of the privatization model and the role of IFIs in promoting such reforms.

The Tanzanian case underscores several critical lessons for water sector privatization efforts, especially in developing countries. It highlights the importance of robust contract management, realistic assessment of investment capabilities, and the need for genuine stakeholder engagement. Moreover, the experience in Dar es Salaam illustrates the challenges of aligning privatization with public interest, particularly in contexts where local governance and institutional capacities are still evolving.

Rationale Behind Conditionalities

The conditionalities imposed by IFIs are grounded in a set of economic theories and beliefs:

1. **Increased Efficiency:** A core argument for privatization is the belief that the private sector, driven by profit motives and competition, operates more efficiently than public entities. This efficiency, it is argued, can lead to better service delivery, reduced waste, and technological innovation.

2. **Attraction of Investment:** By involving the private sector, countries can leverage additional financial resources for infrastructure development and maintenance. Private investment is seen as crucial for bridging the funding gap in the water sector, particularly in developing countries facing fiscal constraints.

3. **Infrastructure Improvement:** The infusion of private capital and expertise is expected to lead to improvements in water infrastructure, enhancing the quality, reliability, and sustainability of water services. This perspective posits that private entities are better positioned to undertake and manage the risks associated with large-scale infrastructure projects.

- The rationale behind these conditionalities reflects a broader ideological shift towards market-based solutions for public service provision. However, the implementation of these policies, particularly in the water sector, has sparked significant debate and controversy. Critics argue that water, as a fundamental human right and a public good, should not be subjected to market forces and profit motives. The case studies of Bolivia and Tanzania, among others, illustrate the potential pitfalls of applying a one-size-fits-all approach to water privatization, highlighting the need for nuanced, context-sensitive policies that prioritize access, affordability, and sustainability.

Impact of IFI Policies on Water Privatization

The influence of International Financial Institutions (IFIs) on the global push for water privatization has been profound, particularly in developing countries. These policies have been pivotal in shaping national approaches to water management, often advocating for privatization as a means to achieve efficiency, enhance service quality, and mobilize investment. However, the outcomes of these efforts have been mixed, with notable successes overshadowed by significant challenges and failures. This section examines the global impact of IFI policies on water privatization, analyzing the successes and failures of these efforts and discussing the critical social and economic consequences.

Successes and Failures of Privatization Efforts

The advocacy of IFIs for water privatization has led to a number of high-profile privatization projects across the globe. In some cases, these projects have resulted in improved efficiency and service delivery, demonstrating the potential benefits of private sector involvement. For instance, in countries with strong regulatory frameworks and clear contractual agreements, privatization has sometimes led to significant investments in infrastructure and technological innovation.

However, the failures of privatization efforts have often been more visible and contentious than the successes. In many developing countries, the promise of privatization has been marred by issues such as:

- **Inadequate Investment:** Contrary to expectations, private companies have sometimes failed to make the necessary investments in infrastructure, leading to deteriorating service quality and reliability.

• **Increased Tariffs:** One of the most common and contentious outcomes of privatization has been the increase in water tariffs. These increases have often placed a significant financial burden on low-income households, exacerbating issues of access and affordability.

• **Reduced Access:** In some cases, the focus on profitability has led to reduced access to water services, particularly for poor and marginalized communities. This has been due to both increased tariffs and a lack of investment in extending services to underserved areas.

Critical Perspectives on the Consequences of Privatization

The mixed outcomes of water privatization efforts have prompted critical examination of the social and economic consequences of these policies. Key concerns include:

• **Social Equity:** The privatization of water services has raised significant concerns about social equity. Increases in tariffs and the prioritization of service delivery to profitable areas have often resulted in unequal access to water, with the poorest segments of the population being the most adversely affected.

• **Economic Burden:** For many households in developing countries, the increased cost of water following privatization represents a significant economic burden. This can lead to difficult trade-offs, with families having to choose between water and other essentials.

- **Public Opposition and Protests:** The adverse effects of privatization have frequently led to public opposition and protests. From the Cochabamba Water War in Bolivia to demonstrations in countries like Tanzania and Indonesia, there has been significant resistance to privatization measures. These protests have often highlighted broader concerns about governance, transparency, and the right to water.

Case Studies of IFI-Influenced Privatization

The push for water privatization, influenced by International Financial Institutions (IFIs) like the World Bank and the International Monetary Fund (IMF), has led to a series of high-profile privatization efforts around the globe. These efforts have varied in their approach, outcomes, and the level of public response they have elicited. Below, we delve into two significant case studies: the Cochabamba Water War in Bolivia and the Manila water privatization in the Philippines. These cases illustrate the complexities and consequences of IFI-influenced water privatization.

Cochabamba Water War, Bolivia

IFI Involvement: The World Bank played a pivotal role in the privatization of Cochabamba's water services. In the late 1990s, the World Bank indicated that it would not renew a

$25 million loan for water projects in the city unless the water services were privatized. This conditionality led the Bolivian government to privatize the city's municipal water supply.

Privatization Process: The process culminated in the government awarding a concession to Aguas del Tunari, a consortium led by International Water Ltd., a subsidiary of the U.S.-based Bechtel Corporation. The contract was signed without a competitive bidding process, and the details were not made public, leading to widespread suspicion and discontent.

Outcomes: Shortly after the privatization, water rates in Cochabamba skyrocketed, in some cases tripling. The high rates made it impossible for many residents to afford basic water services, leading to severe public distress and accusations of mismanagement and corruption.

Public Response: The dramatic increase in water tariffs sparked the Cochabamba Water War, a series of protests that began in January 2000. The protests escalated, resulting in widespread civil unrest, confrontations with the police, and the declaration of martial law. The violence led to several deaths and hundreds of injuries. The public outcry was so intense that the government was forced to cancel the contract with Aguas del Tunari and revert the water services to public control.

Manila Water Privatization, Philippines

IFI Involvement: The privatization of Manila's water services in 1997 was influenced by the Asian Development Bank (ADB) and the World Bank, which advocated for privatization as a solution to the city's water supply and sanitation challenges. The ADB provided technical assistance and played a key role in structuring the privatization process.

Privatization Process: The Metropolitan Waterworks and Sewerage System (MWSS), the government agency responsible for water services in Metro Manila, was privatized through the awarding of two concession contracts. These contracts divided the city into two service areas, with one concession awarded to Manila Water Company, Inc. for the east zone, and the other to Maynilad Water Services, Inc. for the west zone.

Outcomes: The privatization initially led to improvements in water access and service delivery, with significant investments made in infrastructure and expansion of services. However, the process was not without its challenges. Both concessionaires faced financial difficulties, leading to disputes over rate adjustments and concession terms. Maynilad even underwent a rehabilitation process due to its financial troubles.

Public Response: While not as tumultuous as the response in Cochabamba, the Manila water privatization has faced criticism and public protests, particularly over tariff increases and service interruptions. Consumer groups and civil society organizations have repeatedly raised concerns about affordability and the transparency of the rate-setting process.

These case studies underscore the profound impact IFI policies can have on national water privatization efforts. While the IFIs' involvement is often driven by a rationale of improving efficiency and service delivery, the outcomes highlight the complexities of implementing privatization in the water sector.

The cases of Cochabamba and Manila illustrate that without adequate safeguards, transparency, and public engagement, water privatization can lead to significant social unrest and challenges in service provision. These experiences emphasize the need for a careful, context-sensitive approach to water sector reform, one that prioritizes the needs and rights of the population above all.

Critiques and Alternatives to IFI-Driven Privatization

The push for water privatization by International Financial Institutions (IFIs) has been met with significant critique from a broad spectrum of stakeholders, including non-governmental organizations (NGOs), activists, scholars, and affected communities. These critiques often center on concerns related to environmental sustainability, social equity, and governance. In response to these critiques, various alternative models for water management have been proposed and implemented in different contexts, challenging the privatization paradigm promoted by IFIs. Additionally, there has been some shift in the policies and rhetoric of IFIs themselves, reflecting a growing recognition of the complexities of water management and the need for more inclusive and sustainable approaches.

Critiques of IFI-Driven Privatization

Environmental Sustainability: Critics argue that privatization can lead to environmental degradation due to the prioritization of profit over ecological considerations. The focus on short-term financial returns can result in over-extraction of water resources, inadequate investment in sustainable infrastructure, and neglect of the natural ecosystems that replenish water sources.

Social Equity: One of the most vocalized critiques is that privatization often leads to increased water tariffs, making access to clean water unaffordable for low-income households. This exacerbates social inequalities and undermines the human right to water. Furthermore, privatization initiatives have sometimes resulted in the marginalization of communities from decision-making processes regarding the management of their water resources.

Governance: There is also concern that privatization can lead to a lack of transparency and accountability in water management. Contracts between governments and private entities are often negotiated behind closed doors, with little to no public oversight. This can breed corruption and mismanagement, further compromising the quality and accessibility of water services.

Alternative Models for Water Management

In response to the challenges posed by privatization, several alternative models have emerged, emphasizing community involvement, public ownership, and sustainability.

Public-Public Partnerships (PUPs): Unlike privatization, PUPs involve collaboration between public authorities, water utilities, and sometimes non-profit organizations to improve water service delivery. These partnerships leverage the strengths of each party, focusing on knowledge sharing, capacity building, and financial support without relinquishing public ownership and control.

Community-Based Management: This model places the management and governance of water resources directly in the hands of local communities. By empowering communities to manage their water systems, this approach aims to ensure that water management practices are equitable, sustainable, and tailored to local needs and conditions.

Public Trust Approach: The public trust doctrine is a legal principle that regards certain natural resources, including water, as common goods that should be held in trust for public use. This approach argues for the protection of water resources from privatization and exploitation, ensuring that they are managed sustainably for the benefit of current and future generations.

The Role of IFIs in Supporting Sustainable and Equitable Water Management Alternatives

In recent years, there has been a noticeable shift in the policies and rhetoric of some IFIs, partly in response to widespread criticism of their support for water privatization. Institutions like the World Bank have begun to acknowledge the importance of governance, equity, and sustainability in water management. This has led to increased support for initiatives that emphasize community participation, integrated water resources management (IWRM), and investments in public water infrastructure.

- However, the transition towards more sustainable and equitable models of water management requires significant changes in the approach of IFIs. This includes prioritizing grants and loans that support public and community-based water projects, incorporating strict environmental and social safeguards into funding agreements, and fostering transparency and public participation in water management projects.

The exploration of the role of International Financial Institutions (IFIs) in the global movement towards water privatization reveals a complex and multifaceted narrative. IFIs, most notably the World Bank and the International Monetary Fund, have been instrumental in shaping the policies and practices of water management across the globe. Their advocacy for privatization, driven by a belief in the efficiency and innovation of the private sector, has led to significant changes in how water services are delivered and managed. However, the outcomes of these efforts have been mixed, highlighting the challenges and contradictions inherent in applying market-based solutions to the provision of a fundamental human right.

The experiences of countries and communities affected by IFI-influenced water privatization policies offer valuable lessons for the future of global water management. These case studies underscore the importance of considering the social, environmental, and economic dimensions of water services. They reveal that privatization, without adequate safeguards and community engagement, can exacerbate inequalities, undermine access to clean water, and lead to environmental degradation. Conversely, they also show the potential for alternative models of water management that prioritize public ownership, community involvement, and sustainability.

Reflecting on these lessons, it is clear that the path forward requires a reevaluation of the principles and priorities that guide global water management policies. There is a pressing need for approaches that recognize water not merely as an economic commodity but as a shared resource essential for life, ecological health, and human dignity. This calls for a shift away from profit-driven privatization towards more inclusive, equitable, and sustainable models of water governance.

To achieve this vision, a concerted effort from all stakeholders, including governments, IFIs, civil society, and local communities, is necessary. IFIs, in particular, have a critical role to play in this transition. They must leverage their influence and resources to support policies and projects that align with the principles of equity, sustainability, and human rights. This includes providing financial and technical support for public and community-based water management initiatives, incorporating strict environmental and social safeguards into their funding agreements, and fostering transparency and public participation in water governance.

The call to action is clear: the global community must prioritize inclusive, equitable, and sustainable approaches to water management that uphold human rights and protect the environment. As we move forward, the lessons learned from decades of IFI-influenced water policies can guide us towards a future where access to clean water is recognized and realized as a fundamental right for all.

Case Studies of Water Privatization

The narrative of water privatization is rich with examples from across the globe, each illustrating the complex interplay between corporate interests, government policies, and community rights. This section delves into key case studies from Bolivia, South Africa, and India, offering a panoramic view of the varied landscapes of water privatization and the resistance movements it has sparked.

Bolivia's Cochabamba Water War

Privatization Process: The privatization of Cochabamba's water supply in the late 1990s became a textbook example of privatization gone awry. The Bolivian government, encouraged by IFI recommendations and promises of financial support, granted a concession to Aguas del Tunari, a consortium led by the multinational Bechtel Corporation.

Key Players: The key players included the Bolivian government, Aguas del Tunari (Bechtel), and the World Bank. The local population, initially bystanders, soon became central actors in the unfolding drama.

Outcomes: The immediate aftermath of the privatization was a dramatic increase in water prices, which ignited widespread protests in what came to be known as the Cochabamba Water War. The conflict highlighted the tension between privatization's profit motives and the basic human right to water.

Resistance Movements: The resistance was led by a coalition of farmers, factory workers, and everyday citizens. The movement's success in reversing the privatization contract marked a significant victory for public water rights and set a precedent for similar struggles worldwide.

South Africa's Privatization Efforts

Privatization Process: In the post-apartheid era, South Africa embarked on a journey to overhaul its water services, aiming to extend access while grappling with fiscal constraints. This led to a push towards privatization and public-private partnerships, particularly in urban areas like Johannesburg.

Key Players: The South African government, international corporations like Suez and Veolia, and local communities were the primary stakeholders. The involvement of IFIs in advising on these reforms was also notable.

Outcomes: While some improvements in efficiency and infrastructure were observed, the privatization efforts in South Africa were met with challenges, including increased water tariffs and disconnections for non-payment. These measures disproportionately affected the poor, highlighting the social equity issues inherent in privatization.

Resistance Movements: Community groups and NGOs mounted significant resistance, arguing that water is a basic human right. The backlash against privatization efforts underscored the deep divisions in post-apartheid South Africa and the challenges of balancing fiscal sustainability with equitable access to essential services.

India's Struggles with Corporate Water Extraction

Privatization Process: India's encounters with water privatization have often involved large corporations extracting water for bottled water production or industrial use. In several states, companies like Coca-Cola and PepsiCo have been granted licenses to extract vast amounts of groundwater, leading to shortages and pollution.

Key Players: The central and state governments, multinational corporations, local communities, and activist groups have been the main actors in these conflicts.

Outcomes: The extraction of groundwater by corporations in India has led to depleted water tables, reduced access to clean water for local populations, and environmental degradation. These issues are compounded by the lack of stringent regulatory frameworks and enforcement.

Resistance Movements: Local communities, supported by national and international NGOs, have launched campaigns against corporate water extraction. These movements have sometimes resulted in the revocation of corporate licenses and have sparked a broader debate about water governance and corporate responsibility in India.

The resistance movements and public backlash against water privatization efforts across the globe underscore a profound clash between profit motives and the fundamental human right to water. These movements are not merely reactions to policy changes but are emblematic of a deeper struggle for justice, equity, and sustainability in water management. They highlight the tension between viewing water as a commodity to be sold for profit and as a vital resource that should be accessible to all, regardless of economic status.

Bolivia's Cochabamba Water War: A Symbol of Resistance

The Cochabamba Water War is perhaps the most emblematic example of resistance against water privatization. The public uprising was a direct response to the privatization contract that led to skyrocketing water prices, making it unaffordable for a significant portion of the population. The movement was characterized by widespread mobilization, with diverse segments of society coming together to protest against the commodification of their water supply. The success of the Cochabamba resistance, resulting in the reversal of the privatization contract, has since served as a powerful symbol of the potential for community action to challenge and change unjust policies. It underscored the importance of public participation in decisions about natural resources and highlighted the risks of sidelining communities in favor of corporate interests.

South Africa's Struggle for Equitable Water Access

In South Africa, the move towards privatization and the introduction of cost-recovery models for water services sparked significant public outcry, particularly in impoverished communities. The resistance in South Africa was not just against the privatization per se but also against the broader backdrop of inequality and the legacy of apartheid. Protests and legal challenges were mounted against prepaid water meters and disconnections for non-payment, which were seen as measures that discriminated against the poor. The resistance movements in South Africa have emphasized the need for a rights-based approach to water management, one that ensures access to water as a basic human right and not contingent upon the ability to pay.

India's Campaigns Against Corporate Water Extraction

In India, resistance to corporate water extraction has taken various forms, from local protests to legal battles. Communities affected by the depletion of groundwater due to the activities of multinational beverage companies have been at the forefront of these struggles. The campaigns have often highlighted the irony of extracting water in water-stressed areas only to sell it back to the local population at a premium. The resistance in India is a testament to the growing awareness and activism around water rights and the need for sustainable management of water resources. It also reflects the challenges of regulating corporate activities in a way that protects the environment and public interest.

LIQUID GOLD - THE GLOBAL CRISIS OF WATER

Bottled Water: A Symbol of Commodification

The bottled water industry stands as a poignant symbol of the commodification of water, encapsulating the broader issues and debates surrounding this vital resource's transformation into a marketable product. This industry, which has seen exponential growth over the past few decades, serves as a microcosm for examining the complexities and consequences of treating water—a fundamental human need—as a commodity. The journey of bottled water from a niche product to a global phenomenon offers insights into the mechanisms of commodification at play and the implications for society and the environment.

The Rise of Bottled Water

The global bottled water market has burgeoned into a multi-billion dollar industry, driven by a combination of marketing prowess, consumer perceptions, and global trends. Initially, bottled water was a product of convenience and luxury, associated with health, purity, and status. However, over time, it has become a staple in many households worldwide, reflecting broader shifts towards commodification. This shift is not merely about the physical bottling and selling of water but represents a deeper change in how society values and interacts with water.

Marketing Strategies and Consumer Perceptions

The bottled water industry's growth is largely attributed to aggressive marketing strategies that have successfully positioned bottled water as a safer, healthier alternative to tap water. Through sophisticated advertising campaigns, bottled water companies have tapped into public concerns about water quality and health, portraying their products as the epitome of purity and safety. This portrayal has been remarkably effective, even in regions where tap water is safe and highly regulated, leading consumers to opt for bottled water despite the higher cost and environmental impact.

These marketing strategies have not only created a booming market for bottled water but have also contributed to the broader commodification of water. By emphasizing the value of water as a product, these strategies reinforce the notion of water as a commodity that can be bought and sold, rather than a common good or a basic right.

Environmental Impact

The environmental impact of the bottled water industry is a critical aspect of the commodification debate. The production and disposal of plastic bottles contribute significantly to plastic pollution, one of the most pressing environmental challenges of our time. Millions of tons of plastic bottles end up in landfills and oceans each year, causing harm to wildlife and ecosystems. Moreover, the carbon footprint associated with bottling and transporting water over long distances further exacerbates the industry's environmental impact.

Case Studies of Community Impact

The extraction of water for bottling has also raised concerns about the depletion of local water sources and ecological damage. In several communities around the world, large-scale water extraction by bottled water companies has led to conflicts over water rights and access. These cases highlight the tension between the commercial interests of bottled water companies and the needs of local communities, especially in areas where water resources are scarce or under stress.

The bottled water industry

The bottled water industry has experienced unprecedented growth over the last few decades, a phenomenon largely fueled by sophisticated marketing strategies. These strategies have not only created a booming demand for what is essentially a freely available resource but have also shaped consumer perceptions about the safety and health benefits of bottled water compared to tap water. This analysis delves into the marketing tactics used by bottled water companies to drive demand and examines the implications of portraying bottled water as a superior alternative to tap water.

Creating a Perception of Purity and Safety

One of the cornerstone strategies of bottled water marketing involves portraying bottled water as a cleaner, safer, and healthier alternative to tap water. Through advertisements featuring pristine natural springs and mountains, bottled water companies associate their products with purity and untouched nature. This imagery suggests that bottled water is not only free from contaminants but also in its most natural and beneficial form for the human body.

Exploiting Public Water Safety Concerns

Bottled water companies often capitalize on public concerns about municipal water safety, whether arising from actual incidents of contamination or general distrust in public water systems. By highlighting stories of tap water contamination and emphasizing the rigorous filtration and purification processes their products undergo, these companies present bottled water as a risk-free alternative. This strategy effectively exploits consumer fears, driving people towards bottled water even in areas where tap water meets high safety standards.

Health and Lifestyle Association

Another prevalent strategy is associating bottled water with a healthy lifestyle. Advertisements frequently feature athletes and active individuals choosing bottled water, suggesting that it is not only a healthier choice but a necessary part of an active and health-conscious lifestyle. This association extends to the branding of bottled water, with many products emphasizing natural minerals and electrolytes, suggesting additional health benefits beyond hydration.

Convenience and Accessibility

Marketing strategies also emphasize the convenience of bottled water. Portrayed as the ideal choice for on-the-go hydration, bottled water is marketed as the perfect companion for busy lifestyles. This convenience factor, coupled with the widespread availability of bottled water in various retail settings, from vending machines to supermarkets, reinforces its position as a practical and accessible hydration solution.

Environmental Claims

Interestingly, despite the environmental criticism of bottled water, some companies have adopted marketing strategies that highlight their commitment to sustainability. This includes promoting recycling initiatives, using recycled materials in their bottles, or investing in water conservation projects. These strategies aim to mitigate environmental concerns and appeal to environmentally conscious consumers, although they often face accusations of greenwashing.

Implications of Marketing Strategies

The marketing strategies employed by bottled water companies have significant implications. Firstly, they contribute to the commodification of water, transforming it from a basic human right into a branded consumer product. This shift has economic implications, particularly for consumers who spend significantly on bottled water despite having access to safe tap water.

Secondly, the portrayal of bottled water as safer and healthier than tap water undermines public confidence in municipal water systems, potentially diverting attention and resources away from the maintenance and improvement of public water infrastructure. This can have long-term implications for public health and environmental sustainability.

The environmental impact of the bottled water industry is a topic of increasing concern, particularly regarding plastic pollution and the carbon footprint associated with the production, transportation, and disposal of bottled water. As the demand for bottled water has surged globally, so too has the environmental toll, raising significant questions about sustainability and the long-term health of the planet.

Plastic Pollution

One of the most visible and pressing environmental issues associated with bottled water is plastic pollution. Bottled water is predominantly packaged in single-use plastic bottles, which are derived from fossil fuels. Despite efforts to increase the recyclability of these bottles, a significant proportion ends up in landfills, incinerators, or, worse, as litter in natural environments, including oceans, rivers, and landscapes.

- **Contribution to Global Plastic Waste:** The bottled water industry is a major contributor to global plastic waste. Millions of tons of plastic bottles are produced annually, and a substantial amount of this plastic does not get recycled. Instead, it accumulates in the environment, where it can take hundreds of years to decompose, breaking down into microplastics that pose risks to wildlife and ecosystems.

- **Wildlife and Ecosystem Impact:** Plastic bottles and their fragments can be ingested by animals, leading to injury or death. In marine environments, plastic pollution affects a wide range of species, from plankton to seabirds to large marine mammals. Beyond ingestion, plastic pollution also carries toxic pollutants that can leach into soil and water, further harming wildlife and potentially entering the human food chain.

Carbon Footprint

The carbon footprint of bottled water encompasses the entire lifecycle of the bottle, from the extraction of raw materials to manufacture, transportation, and disposal. Each of these stages contributes to the overall greenhouse gas emissions associated with bottled water, making it a significant concern in the context of climate change.

- **Production and Manufacturing:** The production of PET (polyethylene terephthalate) plastic bottles is energy-intensive, requiring significant amounts of fossil fuels. The process releases carbon dioxide (CO_2), a greenhouse gas, contributing to the warming of the planet.

- **Transportation:** Bottled water is often transported long distances from the source to the consumer, including across international borders. The transportation of bottled water by truck, ship, or air freight further adds to its carbon footprint, with emissions contributing to global warming.

- **Refrigeration:** Once it reaches the point of sale, bottled water is frequently stored in refrigerated units until purchase, requiring electricity that may be generated from fossil fuels, depending on the region. This refrigeration process adds to the overall energy consumption and carbon emissions associated with bottled water.

Addressing the Environmental Impact

The environmental impact of the bottled water industry is significant, with two of the most concerning aspects being plastic pollution and the carbon footprint associated with the entire lifecycle of bottled water. These issues not only contribute to global environmental degradation but also challenge the sustainability of water resources and ecosystems worldwide.

Plastic Pollution

Plastic pollution is one of the most visible and pressing environmental impacts of the bottled water industry. The vast majority of bottled water is packaged in single-use plastic bottles made from polyethylene terephthalate (PET), which, despite being recyclable, often ends up in landfills or, worse, polluting oceans and landscapes.

- **Global Waste Crisis:** It's estimated that millions of tons of plastic bottles are produced annually, with a significant portion escaping the recycling loop.

This contributes to the global crisis of plastic pollution, where plastics not only accumulate in landfills but also in natural habitats, affecting terrestrial and marine life.

- **Lifecycle of a Plastic Bottle:** From production to disposal, plastic bottles undergo a journey that impacts the environment at every stage. The production process itself is resource-intensive, requiring large amounts of fossil fuels and water. After their brief use, the disposal phase sees many bottles ending up in environments where they can take up to 450 years or more to decompose, releasing toxic substances and breaking down into microplastics that infiltrate food chains.

Carbon Footprint

The carbon footprint of bottled water encompasses the greenhouse gas emissions from the production, transportation, and refrigeration of bottled water. Each phase contributes significantly to the overall environmental impact of bottled water, making it a less sustainable option compared to tap water.

- **Production and Manufacturing:** The manufacturing of PET bottles is an energy-intensive process that emits a considerable amount of CO_2. Additionally, the extraction and processing of the raw materials required for these bottles further contribute to the carbon footprint of bottled water.

• **Transportation:** Bottled water often travels long distances from the source to the consumer, including international shipments. The transportation of bottled water, whether by road, sea, or air, generates significant CO2 emissions, contributing to global warming and climate change.

• **Refrigeration:** Once it reaches retailers, bottled water is frequently stored in refrigerated units until sold, consuming electricity and contributing further to its carbon footprint. The energy used for refrigeration is often sourced from fossil fuels, compounding the environmental impact.

Mitigation and Alternatives

Addressing the environmental impact of bottled water requires concerted efforts from manufacturers, consumers, and policymakers. Some strategies include:

• **Improving Recycling Rates:** Enhancing the recycling infrastructure and consumer participation in recycling programs can help mitigate plastic pollution. However, recycling alone cannot solve the problem of plastic waste, as it does not address the issue of production.

- **Alternative Packaging:** Some companies are exploring more sustainable packaging options, such as biodegradable plastics, aluminum, or glass, which have a lower environmental impact than PET bottles. However, these materials also have their own environmental footprints that need to be considered.

- **Promoting Tap Water:** Encouraging the consumption of tap water where it is safe to do so can significantly reduce the demand for bottled water. Investing in public water infrastructure to ensure the safety, taste, and accessibility of tap water is crucial in this regard.

- **Consumer Awareness:** Educating consumers about the environmental impact of bottled water and promoting sustainable alternatives can help shift public behavior towards more eco-friendly choices.

The extraction of water for bottling has led to significant environmental and social impacts in various communities around the world. These case studies highlight the consequences of large-scale water extraction for bottling, underscoring the tension between corporate profit motives and the sustainability of local water resources. The depletion of local water sources and the resultant ecological damage have sparked conflicts, legal battles, and ongoing debates about water rights and conservation.

Case Study 1: Plachimada, Kerala, India

In Plachimada, a village in the southern state of Kerala, India, the Coca-Cola Company's bottling plant became the center of controversy due to its excessive extraction of groundwater. The plant, which began operations in 2000, was accused by local residents of depleting the groundwater levels significantly, leading to water scarcity in a region already facing water availability challenges.

Impact on Community and Ecology:

- **Water Scarcity:** The community experienced severe water shortages, affecting agriculture, the primary livelihood of many residents, and leading to a lack of drinking water.

- **Environmental Damage:** The excessive extraction also led to a decrease in water quality, with reports of increased salinity and pollution in remaining water sources, further impacting agriculture and local health.

Response and Outcome:

- After years of protests led by the local community and supported by international activists, the plant was forced to cease operations in 2004. The state government passed a law in 2011 allowing victims to seek compensation, highlighting the conflict between corporate water use and community water rights.

Case Study 2: San Cristóbal de las Casas, Chiapas, Mexico

San Cristóbal de las Casas in Chiapas, Mexico, faced water stress due to the activities of a Coca-Cola bottling plant operated by FEMSA, the largest public bottler of Coca-Cola products in the world. The plant extracted millions of liters of water from local aquifers, leading to tensions over water rights and access.

Impact on Community and Ecology:

- **Depletion of Water Sources:** The bottling plant's high volume of water extraction exacerbated water scarcity in a region where access to potable water is limited, forcing many residents to rely on trucked-in water.

- **Socioeconomic Divide:** The situation highlighted a stark contrast between the water-intensive operations of the bottling plant and the basic needs of the local population, raising issues of environmental justice and equitable water distribution.

Response and Outcome:

- The community organized protests and campaigns against the bottling plant's water use. While the plant continues to operate, the case has drawn attention to the broader issues of corporate water extraction in Mexico and the need for sustainable water management policies that prioritize human and ecological needs.

Case Study 3: Fryeburg, Maine, USA

Fryeburg, Maine, became a battleground over water rights due to Nestlé's Poland Spring brand's operations. The company's extraction of groundwater for bottling sparked legal and community battles, with residents raising concerns about the long-term sustainability of local aquifers.

Impact on Community and Ecology:

- **Legal Battles:** The community engaged in prolonged legal disputes with Nestlé over the company's right to extract water, highlighting the challenges of regulating commercial water bottling activities.

- **Community Mobilization:** Residents and activists mobilized to protect local water sources, advocating for stricter regulations on water extraction and bottling.

Response and Outcome:

- The controversy led to increased awareness and regulatory scrutiny of bottled water operations in

Maine and other parts of the United States. It underscored the need for comprehensive water management policies that consider the cumulative impacts of water bottling on local resources.

Corporate Influence on Policy and Perception

The influence of corporations on public policy and perception, particularly in the context of water rights and access, is a multifaceted issue that has garnered significant attention and concern. Through a combination of lobbying efforts, marketing strategies, and public relations campaigns, corporations have been able to shape policies and public perceptions in ways that often prioritize their interests, sometimes at the expense of public resources and rights. This section investigates the mechanisms through which corporations exert their influence and the implications for water rights and access.

Lobbying and Regulatory Influence

One of the primary avenues through which corporations influence water policy is through lobbying. By engaging in lobbying activities, corporations can sway legislation and regulatory frameworks to favor their business models and operational needs. This can include pushing for favorable water extraction rates, weakening environmental regulations that protect water resources, or influencing the privatization of public water services.

- **Case Example:** In many jurisdictions, beverage and bottling companies have successfully lobbied for low extraction fees and minimal regulation, allowing them to extract groundwater at rates that significantly exceed sustainable levels. This has led to situations where corporate access to water is prioritized over local communities' access to this essential resource.

Marketing Strategies and Public Perception

Corporations also influence public perception through sophisticated marketing strategies that promote bottled water over tap water. By portraying bottled water as a cleaner, safer, and more fashionable choice, these companies create a demand for their products while subtly undermining trust in public water systems.

- **Impact:** This marketing approach not only boosts sales of bottled water but also shifts public perception, leading some to view access to water as a commodity rather than a universal right. This can have long-term implications for public investment in and support for municipal water services.

Public Relations and Community Engagement

Another strategy employed by corporations to influence policy and perception is through community engagement and public relations campaigns. These efforts often aim to present the company as a responsible steward of water resources, even when their practices may contribute to water scarcity and pollution.

- **Case Example:** Some corporations engage in "water stewardship" initiatives that promise to replenish the water they extract or invest in local water infrastructure. While these efforts can have positive outcomes, critics argue they sometimes serve more as a tool for public relations, diverting attention from the broader impacts of their water usage.

Corporate lobbying for favorable water extraction laws, subsidies, and regulations is a global phenomenon, with numerous examples highlighting how companies influence water policy to benefit their operational needs. These efforts often result in policies that allow for extensive water extraction at minimal cost, affecting local ecosystems and community access to water. Here are some notable examples:

Nestlé in California, USA

Nestlé Waters North America (now BlueTriton Brands) faced scrutiny for its water extraction practices in California, particularly during the state's severe droughts. The company extracted millions of gallons of water annually from the San Bernardino National Forest under a permit that had reportedly expired decades ago. Despite public outcry and regulatory challenges, Nestlé continued its extraction, leveraging legal battles and lobbying efforts. Critics argued that the company's influence helped it navigate regulatory loopholes, allowing it to extract water with little oversight or compensation to the public.

Coca-Cola in India

Coca-Cola's operations in India provide another example of corporate lobbying for favorable water policies. In Plachimada, Kerala, and other locations, the company faced opposition due to its groundwater extraction practices, which locals claimed depleted water tables and harmed agricultural livelihoods. Coca-Cola engaged in lobbying and public relations campaigns to maintain its operations, emphasizing its economic contributions and launching community water projects. Despite these efforts, grassroots activism and legal challenges have sometimes forced the company to alter its practices or shut down facilities.

Mining Companies in Chile

Chile's mining sector, crucial to its economy, is another area where corporate lobbying has significantly impacted water regulations. Mining operations in the Atacama Desert, one of the driest places on earth, require vast amounts of water, leading to competition over scarce resources. Companies like BHP and Antofagasta Minerals have lobbied for policies that allow them to access and extract groundwater and surface water for mining operations. These efforts have raised concerns about sustainability and the impact on local communities and ecosystems, prompting calls for stricter water governance.

LIQUID GOLD - THE GLOBAL CRISIS OF WATER

Agribusiness in Brazil

In Brazil, large agribusiness corporations have lobbied for water policies that support the expansion of irrigation for soybean cultivation and other crops, particularly in the Cerrado and Amazon regions. This lobbying has led to regulatory changes that facilitate access to water for agriculture, often at the expense of environmental conservation and indigenous rights. The result is increased stress on water resources in areas already impacted by deforestation and climate change.

Fracking Industry in the United States

The hydraulic fracturing (fracking) industry in the U.S. has successfully lobbied for exemptions from key environmental regulations, allowing it to extract and use large quantities of water for fracking operations. The "Halliburton Loophole" in the Energy Policy Act of 2005, which exempts fracking from certain provisions of the Safe Drinking Water Act, is a prime example of how industry lobbying can lead to favorable regulations that have profound implications for water resources and public health.

The influence of corporate-sponsored research and think tanks on public discourse and policy, particularly regarding the privatization and commodification of water, represents a significant aspect of how corporate interests shape policy environments and public opinion. By funding research and think tanks, corporations can promote narratives that align with their business interests, often emphasizing the benefits of privatization and market-based solutions for water management. This strategy can have profound implications for policy decisions and the broader public understanding of water rights and sustainability.

Promoting Privatization Narratives

Corporate-sponsored research and think tanks frequently produce studies and policy recommendations that advocate for the privatization of water services. These narratives often highlight the supposed inefficiencies of public water management and the potential for private sector involvement to bring investment, innovation, and efficiency to the delivery of water services. By framing privatization as a solution to issues of access and quality, these narratives can influence policymakers and the public to support the transfer of water services to private entities.

Shaping Public Discourse

The dissemination of corporate-sponsored research through media outlets, policy forums, and academic channels plays a crucial role in shaping public discourse on water management. By presenting privatization and commodification as technically and economically rational choices, these narratives can shift public opinion and create a more favorable environment for policy changes that support corporate interests in the water sector. This influence is particularly significant in contexts where public debate on water policy is highly contested and where there is a need for investment in water infrastructure.

Influencing Policy Decisions

Corporate-sponsored think tanks and research organizations often have direct channels to policymakers through lobbying efforts, advisory roles, and participation in policy development processes. The research produced by these entities can inform policy decisions, providing a veneer of academic legitimacy to the push for privatization and commodification. In some cases, the recommendations of corporate-sponsored research have been incorporated into legislation and regulatory frameworks, directly impacting water governance and management practices.

Case Studies and Examples

Several examples illustrate the impact of corporate-sponsored research on water policy:

- **The Global Water Intelligence**, a publication that provides analysis and data on the water market, often highlights the opportunities for private investment in water infrastructure. While offering valuable insights, its coverage can emphasize the benefits of privatization, influencing stakeholders' perceptions and decisions.

- **The World Water Council**, which has partnerships with various private companies, has been criticized for promoting policies that favor privatization in its forums and reports. The Council's role in setting the agenda for global water discussions means that its support for market-based solutions can significantly influence international water policy debates.

- **The Water Initiative of the World Economic Forum**, which involves multiple corporate partners, works on projects and policy recommendations that often highlight the role of the private sector in addressing water challenges. While the initiative supports a range of solutions, its emphasis on public-private partnerships reflects a broader trend towards commodification.

Critiques and Concerns

Critics argue that the influence of corporate-sponsored research on water policy prioritizes profit motives over the public interest, potentially undermining the sustainability and equity of water management. Concerns include the risk of bias in research, the lack of transparency in funding sources, and the potential for conflicts of interest. Moreover, the emphasis on privatization and commodification can divert attention from alternative models of water governance that prioritize community control, public accountability, and the protection of water as a common good.

LIQUID GOLD - THE GLOBAL CRISIS OF WATER

The Human Cost of Commodification

The commodification of water, while often discussed in terms of policy, economics, and environmental impact, bears a profound human cost that can sometimes be overshadowed in broader debates. Behind the statistics and strategic discussions are personal stories of communities and individuals deeply affected by the transformation of water from a shared resource into a commodity. These narratives highlight the human dimension of the water commodification crisis, offering a poignant reminder of what is at stake.

The Story of Maria in Bolivia

Maria, a resident of Cochabamba, Bolivia, found herself at the heart of what would become known as the Cochabamba Water War. When the city's water supply was privatized, and rates soared, Maria, like many others, saw her family's water bill triple. For Maria, whose income barely covered the essentials, this increase meant choosing between water and other critical needs like food and medicine. The privatization, which had promised efficiency and better service, instead brought Maria and her community to the brink of a humanitarian crisis. Their fight against the commodification of their water supply became a symbol of resistance against water privatization worldwide.

Sipho's Struggle in South Africa

In the post-apartheid era, South Africa faced the challenge of extending water services to its entire population. However, the move towards privatization and the introduction of cost-recovery mechanisms placed a heavy burden on impoverished communities. Sipho, living in a township near Johannesburg, experienced firsthand the consequences of these policies. The installation of prepaid water meters in his community meant that access to water was directly tied to one's ability to pay. For Sipho and his neighbors, many of whom were unemployed, this policy led to periods of water scarcity, affecting their health and dignity. The struggle for water access in Sipho's community underscores the social inequities exacerbated by the commodification of water.

A Village in Rajasthan, India

In a small village in Rajasthan, India, the arrival of a large bottling plant promised employment and development. However, the plant's extraction of groundwater led to a rapid depletion of the local water table, affecting agriculture and drinking water supply. For Asha, a farmer in the village, the changes meant the loss of her family's livelihood and a daily struggle to secure enough water for her family's basic needs. The commodification of water, in this case, threatened the very survival of Asha's community, highlighting the conflict between corporate interests and the rights of local populations to their natural resources.

Reflections on the Human Cost

These stories, among countless others, illustrate the profound human cost of water commodification. They reveal the struggles of communities fighting for their right to water in the face of policies and practices that prioritize profit over people.

The impacts of commodification—ranging from increased water scarcity and financial burden to the loss of livelihoods and threats to cultural practices—underscore the need for a more equitable and sustainable approach to water management.

The personal narratives of those affected by water commodification serve as a powerful call to action. They demand a reevaluation of how societies value and manage water, urging a shift towards models that recognize water as a common good essential for life. These stories remind us that behind every policy decision and market trend are individuals and communities whose lives and futures depend on access to clean, affordable water.

The disparity in water access and quality between affluent and impoverished communities, both within nations and globally, starkly illustrates the social inequalities that pervade modern societies. This divide is not merely a matter of geography or climate but is deeply rooted in economic, political, and social structures that determine who gets access to life's most essential resource. An analysis of this disparity reveals a multifaceted crisis that encompasses environmental justice, public health, and human rights.

Global Disparity in Water Access

Globally, the disparity in water access is most evident when comparing high-income countries with low-income countries. In many developed nations, clean and safe water is so ubiquitous that it is often taken for granted. In contrast, in many developing countries, access to safe drinking water remains a significant challenge due to a combination of factors including lack of infrastructure, pollution, and resource mismanagement. According to the World Health Organization (WHO) and UNICEF, billions of people globally lack safe water, sanitation, and handwashing facilities, with the majority living in low- and middle-income countries.

Within-Nation Disparities

Even within nations, stark disparities exist. In affluent urban areas, households often enjoy uninterrupted access to high-quality water. Meanwhile, impoverished communities, including many indigenous and rural populations, frequently face significant challenges in accessing clean water. These disparities are not limited to developing countries; they are also present in developed nations. For example, in the United States, communities like Flint, Michigan, have struggled with lead-contaminated water, highlighting how socio-economic status and race can influence water quality and access.

Factors Contributing to Disparities

Several key factors contribute to the disparities in water access and quality:

- **Economic Inequality:** Wealthier communities can afford the costs associated with securing clean water, including advanced home filtration systems and bottled water, whereas poorer communities cannot. Economic inequality also influences the allocation of public resources, with wealthier areas often receiving more significant investment in water infrastructure.

- **Political Power and Representation:** Communities with more political influence are better positioned to advocate for their needs, including water access. In contrast, marginalized communities often have little say in the decisions that affect their access to water.

- **Infrastructure and Investment:** In many developing countries, the lack of investment in water infrastructure is a significant barrier to improving water access and quality. Even in developed countries, aging infrastructure and insufficient maintenance can lead to water quality issues, disproportionately affecting less affluent communities.

- **Climate Change and Environmental Degradation:** Climate change exacerbates water scarcity and pollution, with the most severe impacts often felt by the poorest communities who are least equipped to adapt. Environmental degradation, including pollution from industrial activities, further compromises water quality, disproportionately affecting marginalized communities.

The Human Right to Water

The disparities in water access and quality highlight the need to recognize and enforce the human right to water. In 2010, the United Nations General Assembly explicitly recognized the right to safe and clean drinking water and sanitation as essential to the realization of all human rights. This recognition underscores the need for global and national efforts to address the inequalities in water access and to ensure that everyone, regardless of their socio-economic status, has access to the water they need to live and thrive.

The commodification of water – treating this essential resource as a commercial product rather than a fundamental human right – plays a significant role in exacerbating social inequalities and contributing to a cycle of poverty and marginalization. This process, driven by market forces and profit motives, often prioritizes access to water for those who can afford to pay, leaving vulnerable populations without adequate access to clean and safe water. The implications of water commodification are profound, affecting not only the immediate availability of water but also broader social, economic, and health outcomes.

Exacerbating Social Inequalities

Water commodification tends to deepen existing social divides. In many parts of the world, the privatization of water services has led to increased water tariffs, making access unaffordable for low-income families. This creates a stark disparity in access to water based on economic status, with wealthier individuals enjoying uninterrupted access to clean water, while poorer communities face scarcity and health risks associated with using contaminated sources.

Moreover, the allocation of water resources often favors industries and agricultural enterprises willing to pay for large volumes of water, further depleting the availability of water for domestic use in nearby impoverished communities. This allocation reflects a broader trend of prioritizing economic activities over basic human needs, a hallmark of commodification that marginalizes the poor.

Contributing to a Cycle of Poverty

Lack of access to clean water has direct economic implications, contributing to a cycle of poverty. For households, the financial burden of purchasing water from private vendors at inflated prices can consume a significant portion of their income, limiting their ability to invest in education, healthcare, and nutrition. For communities, inadequate access to water impedes economic development by constraining agricultural productivity, reducing income-generating opportunities, and increasing healthcare costs associated with waterborne diseases.

The time and labor invested in water collection also have economic consequences, particularly for women and children who bear the brunt of this responsibility in many societies. Hours spent collecting water are hours not spent on education, paid work, or leisure, perpetuating a cycle of educational neglect, reduced economic participation, and entrenched gender inequalities.

Marginalization and Lack of Agency

The commodification of water often results in marginalized communities having little say in the management and distribution of water resources. Decision-making processes tend to be dominated by corporate interests and government entities that may not prioritize the needs of the poor. This lack of agency extends to the inability to influence water pricing, investment in infrastructure, or policies related to water allocation and use.

Communities affected by water commodification frequently find themselves engaged in struggles to assert their water rights, facing legal, economic, and political barriers. These struggles highlight the broader issue of environmental justice, where marginalized populations bear the disproportionate burden of environmental degradation and resource scarcity.

Global Implications and Responses

The global nature of water commodification calls for international responses that recognize the interconnectedness of water rights, social equity, and sustainable development. Initiatives aimed at addressing water commodification and its impacts include advocating for the recognition of water as a human right, promoting community-based water management models, and implementing regulatory frameworks that ensure equitable access to water.

Efforts to counteract the negative effects of water commodification also involve challenging the narratives that support privatization and market-based solutions, emphasizing instead the value of water as a common good essential for life and well-being. These efforts require the collaboration of civil society, governments, international organizations, and communities to create water governance structures that are equitable, sustainable, and responsive to the needs of all, especially the most vulnerable.

Conclusion

The exploration of the human cost of water commodification throughout this chapter has illuminated the profound tension between treating water as a commodity and recognizing it as a fundamental human right. This tension is not merely theoretical but manifests in tangible hardships for communities worldwide, particularly those already marginalized by socio-economic and political factors. The commodification of water exacerbates existing inequalities, placing the most basic necessity for life beyond the reach of millions, and contributing to a cycle of poverty and environmental degradation that threatens future generations.

The case studies and analyses presented underscore the complex interplay between corporate interests that drive water commodification, government policies that enable these practices, and the rights of communities to access clean, affordable water. This interplay often results in policies and practices that prioritize profits over people, undermining efforts to manage water resources sustainably and equitably.

Pathways Forward

Addressing the challenges posed by water commodification requires a multifaceted approach, encompassing policy reform, community action, and global solidarity. Potential pathways forward include:

- **Policy Recommendations:** Governments should implement and enforce policies that prioritize water as a public good. This includes investing in public water infrastructure, regulating water extraction to prevent depletion and pollution, and ensuring that water pricing is fair and equitable. Policies should also recognize the human right to water, embedding this principle in national and international legal frameworks.

- **Community Action:** Communities can play a pivotal role in advocating for their water rights and managing local water resources. Community-based water management initiatives, which involve local stakeholders in decision-making processes, can ensure that water systems meet the needs of all community members. Additionally, grassroots movements can hold corporations and governments accountable for their actions, pushing for changes in policy and practice.

• **Global Solidarity Movements:** The global nature of the water crisis calls for international cooperation and solidarity. Movements aimed at ensuring water access for all can bridge divides between nations, fostering a collective approach to managing water resources sustainably. International organizations, NGOs, and civil society groups can support these movements, amplifying the voices of those most affected by water commodification.

A Call to Action

This chapter serves as a call to action for readers to engage with water rights issues at local, national, and international levels. Whether through supporting community-based water initiatives, advocating for policy changes, or participating in global solidarity movements, everyone has a role to play in addressing the water crisis. Engagement can take many forms, from educating oneself and others about the issues, to participating in advocacy campaigns, to making conscious choices about water use in daily life.

The urgency of ensuring water access for all cannot be overstated. As the global population grows and climate change intensifies, the pressures on water resources will only increase. The time to act is now, to shift the paradigm from water commodification to water as a shared, public resource that is accessible to everyone, regardless of socio-economic status. By recognizing water as a fundamental human right and taking collective action to protect this right, we can work towards a more equitable and sustainable future for all.

Through a comprehensive understanding of the global crisis of water scarcity and pollution, as well as the urgent need for sustainable solutions, readers are equipped to contribute to the vital task of ensuring that water, life's most essential resource, is preserved and accessible for generations to come.

The Politics of Thirst

The Politics of Thirst

Water scarcity has increasingly become a focal point of geopolitical tension and conflict, serving both as a tool for exerting influence and a source of strife between nations, regions, and communities. The politics of thirst encapsulates the complex interplay between natural resource management, political power, and human survival, highlighting how water scarcity is not merely an environmental issue but a profound challenge to global peace and security.

Water Scarcity as a Geopolitical Tool

Nations and entities wielding control over significant water resources often find themselves in positions of considerable power, able to influence regional politics and negotiations. The control of upstream water resources in transboundary river basins, for example, grants countries the ability to regulate the flow of water downstream, impacting agriculture, energy production, and basic water supply in neighboring countries. This control can be leveraged as a geopolitical tool, used to exert pressure or negotiate concessions in broader political or economic disputes.

- **Case Study:** The Nile River dispute among Egypt, Sudan, and Ethiopia over the Grand Ethiopian Renaissance Dam (GERD) exemplifies how water scarcity and control can become central to geopolitical negotiations. Ethiopia's dam has the potential to significantly impact water flow to downstream countries, raising concerns over water scarcity and prompting complex tripartite negotiations over the dam's filling and operation.

Water Scarcity and Conflict

Water scarcity can also be a direct source of conflict, both within and between nations. As water becomes increasingly scarce due to overuse, pollution, and climate change, competition over limited resources can lead to heightened tensions and, in some cases, violence. This is particularly true in regions where water scarcity intersects with existing social, economic, and ethnic divisions, exacerbating grievances and contributing to conflict.

- **Case Study:** In Yemen, water scarcity has been both a cause and consequence of conflict, with battles over water resources exacerbating the country's ongoing humanitarian crisis. Limited access to water has fueled tensions and violence among communities, while the conflict has further degraded the country's water infrastructure, creating a vicious cycle of scarcity and strife.

The Role of International Law and Cooperation

Given the transboundary nature of many water resources, international law and cooperation play crucial roles in mitigating the potential for conflict and leveraging water scarcity as a tool for peacebuilding. Agreements and treaties can provide frameworks for the equitable and sustainable management of shared water resources, reducing the likelihood of conflict and promoting regional stability.

- **Example:** The Indus Waters Treaty between India and Pakistan, brokered by the World Bank in 1960, has provided a durable framework for water sharing between the two countries, despite ongoing tensions in other areas of their relationship. The treaty underscores the potential for water agreements to serve as mechanisms for cooperation and conflict prevention.

The Human Dimension

At the heart of the politics of thirst is the human dimension—communities and individuals whose lives and livelihoods are directly impacted by water scarcity and the geopolitical maneuvers that surround it. The struggle for access to clean, sufficient water is a daily reality for billions, underscoring the need for water scarcity to be addressed not just as a matter of international relations but as a fundamental human rights issue.

Pathways Forward

Addressing the geopolitical challenges of water scarcity requires a multifaceted approach that includes strengthening international water law, promoting cooperative transboundary water management, and integrating water scarcity into broader peace and security strategies. Equally important is the need to address the root causes of water scarcity, including unsustainable water use, pollution, and climate change, through global cooperation and local action.

The impact of agricultural policies, subsidies, and trade agreements on water usage and conservation is profound and multifaceted, influencing how water resources are allocated, used, and managed across the globe. Agriculture is the largest consumer of freshwater resources, accounting for approximately 70% of total global withdrawals. The ways in which agricultural practices are incentivized or regulated through policy and trade agreements have significant implications for both the sustainability of water resources and the health of ecosystems.

Agricultural Policies and Water Usage

Agricultural policies at both national and international levels often determine the allocation of water resources. These policies can encourage practices that either exacerbate water scarcity or promote more sustainable water use:

- **Subsidies for Water-Intensive Crops:** In many regions, government subsidies for water-intensive crops like cotton, rice, and sugarcane encourage farmers to cultivate these crops even in water-scarce areas, leading to significant strain on local water resources. These subsidies can distort market signals and incentivize overuse of water, contributing to depletion of aquifers and lowering of water tables.

- **Irrigation and Infrastructure Support:** Policies that provide support for irrigation infrastructure can have dual impacts. On one hand, they can improve water efficiency and access, enabling more sustainable agricultural practices. On the other hand, if not carefully managed, they can lead to over-irrigation and waterlogging, particularly if subsidies make water artificially cheap for farmers.

Trade Agreements and Water Conservation

Trade agreements also play a crucial role in shaping agricultural water use by determining the flow of agricultural goods across borders. These agreements can either exacerbate water scarcity or contribute to more efficient global water use, depending on their structure and implementation:

- **Virtual Water Trade:** The concept of "virtual water" refers to the water embedded in the production of traded goods. Trade agreements that facilitate the export of water-intensive crops from water-scarce regions to water-abundant regions can lead to unsustainable water use. Conversely, trade can potentially enhance global water sustainability if it allows water-scarce countries to import water-intensive products, thereby reducing domestic water use.

- **Environmental Standards in Trade Agreements:** Some modern trade agreements include provisions for environmental protection and sustainable resource management. These provisions can encourage the adoption of water-saving technologies and practices by making market access contingent on environmental standards, including efficient water use and conservation.

The Role of Technology and Innovation

Policies and trade agreements that encourage technological innovation and the adoption of water-efficient practices can significantly impact water conservation in agriculture. For example, policies that subsidize the adoption of drip irrigation, precision agriculture, and other water-saving technologies can reduce water use while maintaining or even increasing agricultural productivity.

Challenges and Opportunities

The alignment of agricultural policies, subsidies, and trade agreements with sustainable water management goals presents both challenges and opportunities. On the one hand, entrenched interests and short-term economic incentives can drive policies that are at odds with long-term sustainability. On the other hand, there is a growing recognition of the need to integrate water conservation into agricultural policy and trade frameworks as part of broader efforts to address climate change, protect ecosystems, and ensure food security.

Water rights disputes between nations, states, and indigenous peoples highlight the complex interplay of legal, historical, and ethical considerations surrounding access to and control over water resources. These disputes often arise from competing demands for water for agriculture, human consumption, industrial use, and environmental conservation. They are further complicated by the transboundary nature of water, climate change, and historical treaties or agreements that may no longer reflect current realities or understandings of water as a shared resource.

Disputes Between Nations

International water disputes are common in regions where rivers and lakes cross national boundaries. The allocation of water resources in these transboundary water bodies can lead to tensions and conflicts between countries, particularly in arid regions where water is scarce.

- **Example:** The Nile River dispute involves multiple African nations, including Egypt, Sudan, and Ethiopia. The construction of the Grand Ethiopian Renaissance Dam (GERD) on the Blue Nile, a major tributary of the Nile River, has raised concerns in Egypt and Sudan over water scarcity and control. Negotiations have been ongoing to reach an agreement on the operation of the dam and the equitable distribution of water.

Disputes Between States

Within countries, disputes over water rights can arise between different states or provinces, especially in federal systems where subnational entities have significant autonomy over natural resources.

- **Example:** In the United States, the Colorado River is a source of ongoing disputes among the seven states through which it flows. Agreements and compacts that date back to the early 20th century govern the allocation of the river's water. However, prolonged drought, increased demand, and climate change have intensified the competition for water, leading to legal challenges and negotiations for water sharing.

Disputes Involving Indigenous Peoples

Indigenous peoples often find themselves at the center of water rights disputes due to their historical and cultural connections to land and water. These disputes frequently involve the recognition of traditional water rights, access to water for cultural and spiritual practices, and the impacts of development projects on water quality and availability.

- **Example:** In Canada, First Nations communities have been involved in disputes over water rights related to resource extraction projects, hydroelectric dams, and water pollution. The recognition of indigenous water rights and the requirement for consultation and consent for projects affecting water resources are central issues in these disputes.

Pathways to Resolution

Resolving water rights disputes requires a multifaceted approach that considers legal frameworks, historical rights, and the principles of equity and sustainability. Potential pathways to resolution include:

- **International Treaties and Agreements:** For transboundary water disputes, international treaties and agreements that are based on principles of equitable and reasonable utilization, no harm, and cooperation can provide a framework for resolution.

- **Mediation and Arbitration:** Neutral third-party mediation or arbitration can help parties reach an agreement by facilitating dialogue, identifying mutual interests, and proposing equitable solutions.

- **Recognition of Indigenous Rights:** Recognizing and incorporating indigenous water rights into national laws and policies, based on principles of self-determination and traditional knowledge, can address disputes involving indigenous peoples.

- **Integrated Water Resource Management (IWRM):** Adopting IWRM approaches that consider the entire watershed and involve all stakeholders can help address competing demands and promote sustainable water management.

Drying Wells, Rising Tides

Imagine, if you will, a world where water, the very essence of life, plays a game of hide and seek with humanity. On one side of the globe, rivers overflow their banks, while on the other, the ground cracks open, thirsting for just a drop. This, dear readers, is not the plot of a new comedy show but the stark reality of our global water crisis—a situation so ironic it could almost make you laugh, if it weren't so desperately serious.

Welcome to a tale of two hydrations, where water scarcity and abundance exist in a perplexing balance, much like a diet where you're told to eat more cake and less salad. This is the world of "water stress," a term that sounds like what a fish might feel if it had to attend a job interview. But in reality, it's a scientific way to describe regions that are parched not because nature forgot to pay the water bill, but because of a complex cocktail of climate change, over-extraction, pollution, and, let's not forget, human mismanagement. Yes, we humans have a knack for turning even the simplest tasks into a comedy of errors.

Water stress is measured by indicators that sound like a weather forecast from a dystopian novel: "Today, 40% of the global population will experience severe water stress, with a chance of conflict and migration in the afternoon." These indicators give us a global perspective on regions at risk, painting a picture of a planet where water is both a precious commodity and a source of contention.

From the Sahel zone of sub-Saharan Africa, where water scarcity writes a daily script of survival, to the Middle East's river basins, where rivers have become bone-dry actors on a political stage; from India's agricultural heartlands, where water is the main character in an ongoing drama of sustenance, to the American Southwest, where cities stage an elaborate performance of water conservation—water stress is the critical backdrop against which these stories unfold.

So, as we embark on this journey through the geography of thirst, let's keep in mind the irony of our situation. In a world covered by 70% water, it's the remaining 30% that seems to give us the most trouble. But fear not, for every problem, there exists a solution, or at least a humorous anecdote to ease the tension. After all, if we can't laugh at our predicament, we're left with nothing but dry throats and even drier spirits. Let's dive in, shall we?

The Geography of Thirst

In our world's grand theater, where nature and humanity play out their endless dramas, few scenes are as gripping as those scripted by water scarcity. Let's pull back the curtain on some of the globe's most critically thirsty regions, where the plot twists of water scarcity unfold with both predictable regularity and shocking surprise.

Sub-Saharan Africa's Sahel Zone: A Thirsty Earth

Imagine, if you will, a land where the earth cracks open like a poorly rehearsed stage, begging for a drop of moisture to quench its parched lips. This is the Sahel zone of sub-Saharan Africa, a region that could easily win an award for "Best Performance in a Drought." Here, water scarcity isn't just an inconvenient plot twist; it's the main character in a daily struggle for survival. Climate change, with its flair for the dramatic, has intensified traditional dry seasons into prolonged periods of drought, turning once-fertile lands into scenes of ecological despair. The irony? In a land so rich in culture and life, water remains an elusive treasure, locked away by the changing climate and historical mismanagement.

The Middle East's River Basins: Rivers Running Dry

Next, our stage shifts to the Middle East, where ancient rivers once flowed like the lifeblood of civilizations. The Tigris and Euphrates, famed waterways of lore and legend, now find themselves embroiled in a modern tale of depletion. Here, the plot thickens with over-extraction and pollution, as countries vie for control over these dwindling resources. The scene is one of paradoxical abundance and scarcity, where water is both everywhere and nowhere, leading to a narrative rife with conflict and tension. The region's once-mighty rivers, now reduced to trickles in some places, serve as stark reminders of water's central role in both sustaining and dividing communities.

India's Agricultural Heartlands: The Wells Run Dry

In India's vast agricultural heartlands, water scarcity plays the villain in an epic saga of survival. Groundwater, the unseen hero of past decades, is being drawn upon as if it were an inexhaustible prop. But as wells run dry, the reality of the situation takes center stage: there's no understudy waiting in the wings. Over-extraction, coupled with inefficient water management practices, has turned bountiful areas into scenes of agricultural tragedy. The irony here is palpable—water, so vital for the sustenance of life, becomes a source of strife and division, turning neighbor against neighbor in the quest for the last drops.

The American Southwest: A Mirage of Abundance

Finally, our journey takes us to the American Southwest, a region that stages an elaborate illusion of water abundance. Cities like Phoenix and Las Vegas play their parts well, adorned with fountains and lush greenery, yet backstage, the reality is far different. The Colorado River, the lifeline of the Southwest, is stretched to its limits, its waters allocated in a script written a century ago, without forethought for climate change's dramatic entrance. Here, water scarcity is both a natural and a man-made phenomenon, a reminder that even in the wealthiest nations, water cannot be taken for granted.

Curtain Call

As the curtain falls on these regions, the message is clear: the geography of thirst is vast and varied, yet the underlying themes are universal. Water scarcity, driven by climate change, over-extraction, pollution, and inefficient management, demands a global audience's attention. The stories of these regions, though fraught with challenges, also contain glimmers of hope—innovative solutions, community resilience, and international cooperation can rewrite the script, turning a tale of scarcity into one of sustainable abundance.

Climate Change: The Scene Setter

Climate change acts as the scene setter in this drama, altering weather patterns, intensifying droughts, and reducing rainfall in already arid regions. In the Sahel zone, for instance, climate change has turned seasonal dry spells into prolonged droughts, decimating crops and livestock. Similarly, in the American Southwest, rising temperatures and changing precipitation patterns have reduced river flows, shrinking reservoirs that cities and agriculture rely upon. Climate change's role is insidious, slowly but surely exacerbating water scarcity and setting the stage for more dramatic crises.

Over-Extraction: The Plot Thickens

As the plot thickens, over-extraction enters, driven by the demands of agriculture, industry, and growing populations. In India's agricultural heartlands, the Green Revolution's legacy of high-yield crops has come at the cost of massive groundwater depletion, with wells running dry and farmers left in despair. The Middle East's river basins, too, have been tapped beyond their means, as nations extract water without heed to sustainability, leading to rivers that sometimes run dry before reaching the sea.

Pollution: The Dark Twist

Pollution delivers a dark twist, contaminating the scarce water that remains. Industrial runoff, untreated sewage, and agricultural chemicals taint rivers and groundwater, rendering them unsafe for consumption or agriculture. In sub-Saharan Africa, waterborne diseases flourish in polluted waters, affecting human health and child mortality rates. The irony is cruel: in regions desperate for water, what little is available can often bring death instead of life.

Inefficient Water Management: The Misguided Director

Inefficient water management acts as the misguided director of this play, often exacerbating the crisis through poor planning, corruption, and lack of investment in infrastructure. Age-old irrigation techniques that waste water, subsidies that encourage the growth of water-intensive crops in arid areas, and a lack of regulation on industrial water use all contribute to the problem. This inefficiency turns a manageable issue into a dire crisis, with vulnerable populations bearing the brunt of the consequences.

The Socio-Economic Consequences: The Human Cost

The impact of water scarcity on agriculture, human health, and regional stability is profound, particularly for vulnerable populations. Agriculture, the lifeblood of many of these regions, suffers as fields turn barren, leading to food insecurity and loss of livelihoods. Human health is compromised, not just by the lack of drinking water, but by the diseases that proliferate in scarce and polluted water supplies. Regional stability is threatened as communities, and nations clash over dwindling resources, with water scarcity acting as a catalyst for migration and conflict.

Floods Amidst Drought

In a world grappling with the complexities of climate change, the paradox of increased flooding amidst severe water scarcity presents a confounding subplot in the broader narrative of the global water crisis. This phenomenon, where regions experience both extreme drought and devastating floods, underscores the unpredictable and often ironic impacts of climate change on water resources. Through the lens of case studies from Bangladesh, Venice, and coastal cities in the United States, we explore this paradox and its implications for communities, ecosystems, and water management strategies.

Bangladesh: The Dual Threat of Drought and Monsoons

Bangladesh, cradled by the mighty rivers of the Ganges, Brahmaputra, and Meghna, faces an acute embodiment of this paradox. During the dry season, vast swathes of the country experience water scarcity, affecting agriculture and drinking water supplies. Yet, the monsoon season brings a dramatic reversal, with excessive rainfall leading to widespread flooding. This cycle of drought and flood is exacerbated by climate change, which intensifies monsoon rains and shifts rainfall patterns, making water management a Sisyphean task.

The impact on agriculture, a cornerstone of Bangladesh's economy, is profound. Farmers oscillate between battling drought-induced water shortages that threaten crops and mitigating floodwaters that inundate fields. The human toll is equally severe, with communities displaced and livelihoods destroyed, illustrating the stark vulnerability of water-stressed regions to flooding.

Venice: Rising Tides and Sinking Solutions

Venice, Italy's storied city of canals, presents a unique case of flooding amidst scarcity. Acqua alta, or high water, events have become more frequent and severe, flooding the historic city and highlighting the challenges of managing water in an era of rising sea levels. The irony in Venice's situation lies in its struggle to preserve its aquatic heritage while combating the very element that defines it.

Efforts to mitigate flooding, such as the MOSE project—a system of mobile barriers designed to protect the city from high tides—reflect the complex interplay between human ingenuity and nature's unpredictability. Yet, these solutions do not address the underlying issues of climate change and sea-level rise, underscoring the need for comprehensive approaches that consider both immediate threats and long-term sustainability.

Coastal Cities in the United States: A Convergence of Extremes

Coastal cities in the United States, from Miami to New Orleans, face the dual challenges of drought and flooding. These cities, situated in regions prone to hurricanes and rising sea levels, must navigate the complexities of water management in an era of climate extremes. Hurricane-induced floods devastate infrastructure and communities, while periods of drought strain water supplies and exacerbate competition for resources.

The paradox of floods amidst drought in these cities highlights the broader issue of climate resilience and the need for adaptive water management strategies. It also raises questions about equity and access, as vulnerable populations often bear the brunt of climate impacts, from water scarcity to flood damage.

Scientific Explanation of Climate Change's Impact on Droughts and Floods

Climate change, driven by the accumulation of greenhouse gases in the Earth's atmosphere, is altering weather patterns in profound ways, contributing to both extreme droughts and floods. The science behind these phenomena is rooted in the basic principles of atmospheric physics and hydrology.

- **Warming Atmosphere:** A warmer atmosphere increases the rate of evaporation from soil and water bodies, exacerbating drought conditions in many regions. This increased evaporation also means that the atmosphere can hold more moisture—about 7% more for every 1°C increase in temperature, according to the Clausius-Clapeyron relation. When conditions are right for precipitation, this additional moisture can lead to more intense and frequent rainfall events, contributing to flooding.

• **Melting Ice Caps and Glaciers:** The warming climate is causing ice caps and glaciers to melt at unprecedented rates, contributing to rising sea levels. This not only increases the risk of coastal flooding but also affects freshwater resources. As glaciers retreat, they alter the seasonal flow of rivers they feed, initially increasing water flow but eventually leading to reduced river volumes as the source of the water diminishes.

• **Shifts in Weather Patterns:** Climate change is also altering global weather patterns, including the jet stream and ocean currents, which can lead to prolonged periods of dry or wet weather. For instance, changes in the El Niño Southern Oscillation (ENSO) can influence drought and flood patterns across the globe.

Challenges in Managing Water Resources

The dual threats of extreme drought and flooding present significant challenges for water resource management.

Traditional water management strategies, designed for more predictable and stable climate conditions, are often inadequate to address the current era of climate extremes.

- **Infrastructure Stress:** Existing water infrastructure, including dams, levees, and reservoirs, may be ill-equipped to handle the increased variability and extremes in water availability. For example, reservoirs may not have the capacity to capture and store increased runoff from heavy rainfall events, while also needing to maintain sufficient water levels during prolonged droughts.

- **Water Quality Concerns:** Extreme weather events can exacerbate water quality issues. Floods can lead to contamination of water supplies with pollutants and pathogens, while droughts can concentrate pollutants in water bodies, affecting both human health and ecosystems.

- **Socio-Economic Impacts:** The unpredictability of water availability affects agriculture, energy production, and urban water supply, with significant socio-economic consequences. Vulnerable communities often bear the brunt of these impacts, exacerbating existing inequalities.

Adaptive and Resilient Water Management Strategies

Addressing the challenges posed by climate change requires adaptive and resilient water management strategies that can accommodate the increased variability and extremes in water availability.

- **Integrated Water Resources Management (IWRM):** IWRM approaches emphasize the coordinated management of water, land, and related resources to maximize economic and social welfare without compromising the sustainability of vital ecosystems.

- **Green Infrastructure:** Implementing green infrastructure solutions, such as wetlands restoration and green roofs, can enhance water retention and reduce runoff, mitigating both drought and flood risks.

- **Flexible Policy Frameworks:** Water management policies need to be flexible and adaptive, incorporating mechanisms for responding to changing conditions. This includes revising water allocation priorities, investing in water-saving technologies, and enhancing water-sharing agreements.

- **Community Engagement and Education:** Engaging communities in water management decisions and promoting water conservation practices can enhance resilience to water-related climate extremes.

Personal Narratives of Water Crisis

These stories, drawn from various parts of the world, illustrate the deeply personal and community-level impacts of water scarcity and flooding, offering insights into the resilience and adaptability of those affected.

The Farmer in Maharashtra, India

In the agricultural heartlands of Maharashtra, India, a farmer named Vijay faces the dual challenge of drought and erratic monsoon seasons. Maharashtra has been experiencing severe drought conditions for several years, significantly impacting agricultural productivity and leading to a crisis for farming communities. Vijay's narrative includes the struggle to maintain crops with dwindling water supplies and the financial burden of investing in private wells and expensive irrigation systems. The situation is exacerbated when the monsoons do arrive, as the intense rainfall leads to flooding, destroying crops and further depleting soil quality. Vijay's story is a testament to the struggle of balancing the immediate needs for water with the long-term sustainability of farming practices in the face of climate change.

SOPHIA FAIRVIEW

A Resident of Flint, Michigan, USA

April's story from Flint, Michigan, highlights the human impact of water pollution and mismanagement in a developed country. In 2014, Flint's water source was switched to the Flint River without adequate treatment, leading to lead contamination in the drinking water. April, a mother of two, recounts the confusion and fear that gripped the community as people learned about the contamination. Her narrative includes the frustration with governmental inaction, the fear for her children's health, and the community's fight for clean water. April's experience underscores the critical importance of safe and clean water access and the devastating consequences when it is compromised.

A Family in Dhaka, Bangladesh

In Dhaka, Bangladesh, a family navigates the challenges of living in one of the world's most flood-prone areas. As climate change intensifies the monsoon season, flooding has become more frequent and severe, inundating homes and disrupting lives. The family's story includes the loss of personal belongings, the struggle to find clean drinking water during floods, and the constant threat of waterborne diseases. Their narrative also touches on the broader socio-economic impacts of flooding, including missed workdays, disrupted education for children, and the strain on local infrastructure. Despite these challenges, the family speaks to the resilience of their community and the collective efforts to adapt to an increasingly unpredictable climate.

LIQUID GOLD - THE GLOBAL CRISIS OF WATER

Farmers in Sub-Saharan Africa: The Struggle Against Drought

In the arid landscapes of sub-Saharan Africa, farmers like Amare in Ethiopia face the relentless challenge of drought. Years of insufficient rainfall have depleted water sources, turning once-fertile fields into barren lands. Amare's narrative is one of adaptation and survival, as he shifts from traditional crops to drought-resistant varieties and employs water-saving irrigation techniques. Despite these efforts, the uncertainty of water availability looms large, threatening food security and livelihoods. Amare's story is a testament to the resilience of rural communities in sub-Saharan Africa, who continue to farm and support their families against increasingly insurmountable odds.

Families in the Middle East: Navigating Water Shortages

In Jordan, one of the world's most water-scarce countries, families like Hala's navigate the daily realities of water shortages. In her narrative, Hala describes the routine of water rationing, where water is supplied only once a week, forcing families to store water in tanks and ration it carefully. The scarcity of water affects every aspect of life, from cooking and cleaning to personal hygiene. Hala's story highlights the ingenuity and resourcefulness of communities in the Middle East as they adapt to life with limited water resources, all while facing the broader challenges of regional instability and displacement.

Residents of Flood-Prone Areas in Asia: Living with Excess Water

In Bangladesh, a country crisscrossed by rivers and prone to monsoons, residents like Fahim experience the paradox of living with both water scarcity and excess. Fahim's family, residing in a low-lying area of Dhaka, faces annual flooding that inundates their home, contaminates drinking water, and spreads disease. The narrative captures the disruption caused by flooding, from displacement to the loss of possessions and the struggle to access clean water. Fahim's story reflects the broader challenges faced by flood-prone communities in Asia, where climate change exacerbates the frequency and severity of flooding, disrupting lives and livelihoods.

Communities in the United States: Coping with Scarcity and Excess

In California, communities navigate the dual challenges of drought and flooding, a reflection of the state's complex water landscape. Maria, a resident of the Central Valley, shares her experience of water scarcity impacting agriculture, the region's economic backbone, leading to job losses and food insecurity. Conversely, heavy rains bring the threat of flooding, damaging homes and infrastructure. Maria's narrative underscores the challenges of managing water resources in an environment of extremes, highlighting the importance of sustainable water practices and infrastructure resilience.

LIQUID GOLD - THE GLOBAL CRISIS OF WATER

Mismanagement and Missed Opportunities

Ah, the human saga of water management, a tale as old as time, filled with twists, turns, and the occasional face-palm moment. In this chapter of our global water narrative, we dive into the murky waters of mismanagement and missed opportunities, where the comedy of errors isn't quite so funny when the stakes are as high as ensuring everyone gets a fair sip from Earth's tap.

The Comedy of Errors: Poor Planning

Imagine, if you will, a group of city planners, gathered around a table that's probably too big, with cups of coffee that are definitely too small. They're tasked with designing a water management system for an ever-growing population, a challenge akin to fitting a square peg in a round hole, if both the peg and hole were constantly moving. In some cases, these well-intentioned plans resemble more of a Rube Goldberg machine than a practical solution, leading to systems that are either overburdened, underprepared for climate extremes, or, in a twist that would be hilarious if it weren't so tragic, both.

The Villain of Our Story: Corruption

Enter the villain of our story, corruption, twirling its metaphorical mustache as it diverts funds, resources, and opportunities away from where they're desperately needed. In some regions, the allocation of water rights and resources becomes a backstage pass, available only to those with the right connections or deep enough pockets. This not only exacerbates scarcity but also ensures that the stage is set for a performance where the rich get richer, and the poor get thirstier.

The Missed Cue: Lack of Investment in Infrastructure

And then, there's the missed cue, the lack of investment in infrastructure. Picture a network of pipes, canals, and treatment plants that haven't seen an upgrade since the audience was wearing bell-bottoms and disco was king. Leakage, contamination, and inefficiency are the hallmarks of these aging systems, leading to water loss that's both literal and metaphorical. It's as if we're trying to stream the latest blockbuster over dial-up internet—a lot of buffering, frustration, and ultimately, giving up and going to bed.

The Plot Twist: Adaptive and Resilient Strategies

But fear not, dear reader, for every story has its heroes, and in this tale, it's the innovative minds and resilient communities that are writing the next chapters. From rainwater harvesting in urban jungles to reviving ancient water conservation techniques in arid landscapes, people are finding ways to turn the page on water mismanagement. These adaptive strategies are the plot twists we've been waiting for, offering hope that perhaps, in the end, we can all enjoy a happy ending.

In the realm of water management, the line between success and failure often hinges on a complex interplay of planning, execution, and adaptation. By examining case studies of both failed projects and triumphant initiatives, we can distill valuable lessons to guide future endeavors. Let's embark on a journey through these instructive tales, with just a sprinkle of Hape Kerkeling's wit to keep our spirits buoyed.

Failed Water Management Projects

The Aral Sea Disaster

What Went Wrong: Once the fourth-largest lake in the world, the Aral Sea, located between Kazakhstan and Uzbekistan, has now shrunk to a fraction of its original size. The root cause? Soviet-era water diversion projects aimed at irrigating arid lands for cotton cultivation. This massive engineering feat failed to account for the ecological balance, leading to a catastrophic reduction in water inflow to the sea.

Lessons Learned: The Aral Sea disaster teaches us the importance of holistic environmental assessment in water management projects. It underscores the need for sustainable practices that consider the long-term ecological balance, rather than short-term agricultural or economic gains.

Successful Water Management Initiatives

Singapore's NEWater Program

What Went Right: Facing a scarcity of natural water resources, Singapore turned to technology and innovation to secure its water future. The NEWater program, launched in the early 2000s, recycles treated wastewater into ultra-clean, high-grade reclaimed water. This initiative now meets up to 40% of the nation's water needs, with plans to increase this to 55% by 2060.

Lessons Learned: Singapore's success with NEWater illustrates the potential of technology and innovation in addressing water scarcity. It also highlights the importance of public trust and acceptance in the implementation of new water management solutions, achieved through rigorous safety standards and transparent communication.

The Middle Ground: California's Water Bank

The Scenario: California's Water Bank was established as a response to the state's cyclical droughts, allowing water to be stored in wet years and distributed in dry ones. While the concept is sound, the implementation has faced challenges, including issues with infrastructure, environmental concerns, and the complexities of water rights.

Lessons Learned: The mixed results of California's Water Bank point to the necessity of flexible and adaptive water management systems that can respond to changing conditions and stakeholder needs. It also emphasizes the need for robust infrastructure and clear legal frameworks to support innovative water management strategies.

In the quest to address the global water crisis, innovation and technology play pivotal roles, offering promising solutions for water conservation, recycling, and management. These advancements range from high-tech treatment processes to simple, community-driven conservation techniques. However, the path to widespread implementation of these solutions is often fraught with barriers, both technical and socio-economic.

Innovative Solutions and Technologies

• Smart Irrigation Systems

Overview: Utilizing sensors and IoT (Internet of Things) technology, smart irrigation systems optimize water use in agriculture by adjusting watering schedules based on soil moisture levels, weather predictions, and plant water requirements. This precision agriculture can significantly reduce water wastage.

• Wastewater Recycling and Reuse

Overview: Advanced treatment technologies, such as membrane bioreactors (MBRs) and reverse osmosis, enable the recycling of wastewater to potable standards. Singapore's NEWater and the Orange County Groundwater Replenishment System in California exemplify how treated wastewater can supplement drinking water supplies.

• Atmospheric Water Generation

Overview: Atmospheric water generation (AWG) technology extracts water from humid ambient air. While energy-intensive, recent advancements have made it a viable option for providing clean water in arid regions without depleting groundwater resources.

- **Rainwater Harvesting**

Overview: Simple yet effective, rainwater harvesting systems collect and store rainwater for later use. This low-tech solution can be implemented at various scales, from residential to community levels, reducing dependence on groundwater and surface water.

Barriers to Implementation

Despite the potential of these innovative solutions, several barriers hinder their widespread adoption:

High Initial Costs

The upfront investment required for advanced water treatment and conservation technologies can be prohibitive, especially for developing countries and small-scale farmers. The cost of installing smart irrigation systems or wastewater recycling plants, for instance, may be beyond the reach of those who would benefit most.

Lack of Infrastructure

In many regions, the infrastructure needed to support advanced water management solutions is lacking. This includes not only physical infrastructure like pipes and treatment facilities but also the regulatory and institutional frameworks necessary for effective water governance.

Energy Requirements

Some water conservation and recycling technologies, such as AWG and desalination, are energy-intensive, raising concerns about their carbon footprint and sustainability. The challenge lies in balancing water and energy needs, ideally integrating renewable energy sources into these systems.

Public Perception and Acceptance

Public perception can significantly impact the adoption of certain water management solutions, particularly those involving non-traditional water sources. For example, the "yuck factor" associated with recycled wastewater can deter its acceptance, despite rigorous treatment processes ensuring its safety.

Knowledge and Capacity Building

A lack of awareness and technical expertise can also be barriers to the adoption of innovative water management solutions. Training and capacity-building efforts are essential to equip water managers and communities with the knowledge to implement and maintain these systems effectively.

The Ripple Effects of Water Crisis

The water crisis, characterized by both scarcity and flooding, sends ripples across the fabric of societies, economies, and ecosystems, affecting millions of lives and the stability of nations. The broader implications of these water-related challenges are profound, touching on migration, conflicts, and global food security, among other areas. Understanding these ripple effects is crucial for developing comprehensive strategies to mitigate the impacts and address the root causes of the water crisis.

Migration

Water scarcity and flooding act as powerful drivers of migration, compelling individuals and communities to leave their homes in search of more secure living conditions. In regions afflicted by severe droughts, such as parts of sub-Saharan Africa, the lack of water for drinking, agriculture, and livestock sustenance forces people to move to urban areas or across borders, often leading to overcrowded cities and increased strain on urban infrastructure and resources. Conversely, areas experiencing chronic flooding, like certain river deltas in Asia, see populations relocating to escape the immediate dangers of inundation and the long-term impacts on their livelihoods. This migration can exacerbate existing social and economic tensions and contribute to the complexity of regional and international migration patterns.

Conflicts Over Water Resources

As water becomes increasingly scarce, competition over access to this vital resource can lead to conflicts at various levels. At the local level, disputes may arise between farmers over irrigation rights or between communities over access to drinking water sources. Nationally and regionally, tensions can escalate over the management of transboundary rivers and aquifers, as seen in the disputes over the Nile, Tigris-Euphrates, and Indus River basins. These conflicts not only strain diplomatic relations but also divert resources away from development and poverty alleviation efforts, further entrenching cycles of poverty and instability.

Impacts on Global Food Security

Water scarcity directly impacts agricultural productivity, which in turn affects global food security. Agriculture consumes the largest share of freshwater resources, and the availability of water for irrigation is critical for food production. In areas experiencing water scarcity, crop yields can decline dramatically, leading to food shortages, increased prices, and greater food insecurity. Flooding, on the other hand, can destroy crops, degrade soil quality, and disrupt planting and harvesting cycles, further exacerbating food supply challenges. The ripple effects of these impacts are felt globally, as countries dependent on food imports from affected regions face increased vulnerability to food price volatility and supply disruptions.

The water crisis is not an isolated phenomenon but is deeply intertwined with several other global challenges, including poverty, gender inequality, and education. The intricate connections between these issues amplify the impacts of water scarcity and flooding, creating a complex web of socio-economic and environmental challenges that require holistic and integrated solutions.

Water Crisis and Poverty

The link between water scarcity and poverty is both direct and profound. Access to clean and sufficient water is a fundamental driver of economic development and a basic necessity for human health and well-being. In regions where water is scarce, agriculture—the primary source of income for many rural communities—suffers, leading to food insecurity and reduced incomes. Moreover, the time and resources spent on obtaining water from distant sources detract from opportunities for education and employment, perpetuating cycles of poverty. Flooding, on the other hand, can destroy homes and livelihoods, pushing already vulnerable populations further into poverty.

Water Crisis and Gender Inequality

Gender inequality is both a cause and consequence of the water crisis. In many cultures, the responsibility of collecting water falls disproportionately on women and girls, who may spend several hours each day fetching water from distant sources. This not only exposes them to potential safety risks but also limits their opportunities for education, employment, and participation in community decision-making. Furthermore, the lack of access to safe sanitation facilities, especially during menstruation, can further marginalize women and girls, affecting their health and preventing them from attending school or work.

Water Crisis and Education

The availability of clean water and sanitation facilities is closely linked to educational outcomes. Schools without access to safe water and sanitation are less likely to attract and retain students, particularly girls. The time children spend collecting water or the illnesses caused by waterborne diseases can lead to absenteeism and high dropout rates, undermining educational achievements. Moreover, education plays a crucial role in addressing the water crisis, as it equips individuals with the knowledge and skills needed to implement sustainable water management practices and advocate for their rights to water and sanitation.

Bridging the Gaps

Addressing the water crisis requires acknowledging and tackling these interconnected challenges. Efforts to improve water access and management can have far-reaching benefits for poverty alleviation, gender equality, and education. For instance, investments in water infrastructure can free up time for women and children, allowing them to pursue education and economic activities. Similarly, education programs focused on water conservation and hygiene can improve health outcomes and empower communities to advocate for sustainable water policies.

Moreover, policies and programs aimed at addressing the water crisis must be designed with an understanding of these linkages. For example, initiatives that involve women in water management decisions can lead to more equitable and effective outcomes. Similarly, integrating water, sanitation, and hygiene (WASH) programs into schools can support educational attendance and achievement, particularly for girls.

The international response to the water crisis has been multifaceted, involving a combination of aid, development projects, and the establishment of global agreements aimed at improving water access, management, and conservation. These efforts reflect the growing recognition of water's critical role in sustainable development, public health, and global security. Here's an overview of how the international community is addressing the water crisis:

Aid and Development Projects

Numerous international organizations, governments, and NGOs have launched aid programs and development projects to tackle various aspects of the water crisis. These initiatives range from infrastructure development and technological innovation to capacity building and education programs. For example:

- **The World Bank** has funded numerous projects aimed at improving water supply and sanitation facilities in developing countries, enhancing water resource management, and supporting irrigation for agriculture.

- **UNICEF's WASH (Water, Sanitation, and Hygiene) programs** focus on providing safe drinking water, sanitation, and hygiene education to communities in need, particularly in emergency situations and disaster zones.

• **The Water Project** and **charity: water** are examples of NGOs that work to bring clean and safe drinking water to people in sub-Saharan Africa through community-driven projects.

Global Agreements on Water Management

Global agreements and frameworks play a crucial role in guiding international efforts and promoting cooperation on water issues. These include:

• **The Sustainable Development Goals (SDGs):** Adopted by all United Nations Member States in 2015, the SDGs include Goal 6, which aims to "ensure availability and sustainable management of water and sanitation for all" by 2030. This goal encompasses targets on drinking water, sanitation, water quality, efficiency, integrated water resources management, and ecosystem protection.

• **The United Nations Watercourses Convention:** Entered into force in 2014, this international treaty provides a comprehensive framework for the equitable and reasonable utilization of international watercourses, promoting cooperation and sustainable development.

- **The Ramsar Convention on Wetlands:** This intergovernmental treaty, adopted in 1971, aims to conserve and use wetlands wisely through local, regional, and national actions and international cooperation.

Challenges and Criticisms

Despite these efforts, the international response to the water crisis faces several challenges and criticisms. These include:

- **Funding and Resource Allocation:** Adequate funding remains a significant challenge, with many projects struggling to secure the financial resources needed for long-term sustainability.

- **Coordination and Efficiency:** With numerous actors involved in water crisis response, coordination can be challenging, leading to inefficiencies and overlapping efforts.

- **Equity and Access:** Ensuring that aid and development projects reach the most vulnerable populations and do not exacerbate existing inequalities is a constant concern.

- **Climate Change:** The exacerbating effect of climate change on water scarcity and flooding complicates efforts to manage water resources sustainably, requiring adaptive strategies that can evolve in response to changing conditions.

And so, dear readers, we find ourselves at the end of this watery tale, a journey through the ebb and flow of the global water crisis. It's been a bit like a river cruise, hasn't it? Only instead of sipping cocktails on the deck, we've been navigating the rapids of water scarcity, pollution, and the occasional flood. But what a voyage it's been, offering us a panoramic view of the challenges and triumphs in the world of water management.

We've seen that the issues of water scarcity and abundance are as intertwined as the roots of a mangrove tree. From the parched fields of sub-Saharan Africa to the flooded streets of Bangladesh, the message is clear: our water woes are a shared saga, requiring not just a village but a whole planet to solve. It's a bit like a potluck dinner – everyone needs to bring something to the table, be it innovative solutions, robust policies, or simply a commitment to conserve water in our daily lives.

To our policymakers, consider this a gentle nudge (or a friendly shove) towards prioritizing water sustainability. The policies you craft today are the seeds of tomorrow's water security. To communities around the globe, your actions and advocacy are the lifeblood of change, proving time and again that when people come together, even the driest of deserts can bloom. And to individuals, remember that every drop counts. Your choices, from fixing that leaky faucet to supporting water-wise policies, ripple across the water's surface, contributing to a wave of change.

Let's not forget the power of personal stories and grassroots movements. They're the heartbeats behind the statistics, reminding us that behind every dry well or flooded home, there are faces, families, and futures at stake. These stories are the wind in our sails, propelling us forward, inspiring action, and fostering a sense of global camaraderie in the face of adversity.

In crafting this chapter, we've woven together the threads of scientific analysis, investigative reporting, and heartfelt narratives to create a tapestry that reflects the complex nature of the global water crisis. It's our hope that this exploration has not only enlightened but also ignited a spark within you. A spark to question, to care, and to act. For in the end, the future of water is not just a matter of policy or technology but of humanity itself.

So, as we bid adieu to this chapter, let's carry forward the lessons learned, the inspiration gleaned, and the determination kindled. Together, navigating the changing global water landscape, we can turn the tide of the water crisis, ensuring a sustainable and equitable water future for all. After all, in the grand narrative of our planet, water is the ink in which our story is written. Let's make it a story of hope, resilience, and unity.

Toxic Flows

In the intricate web of life, water serves as the bloodstream of our planet, a vital conduit for nutrients, life, and energy. Yet, this life-giving resource is under siege, tainted by the very civilizations it nurtures. This chapter delves into the murky depths of water pollution, exploring the primary culprits: industrial waste, agricultural runoff, and urban sewage. Through this exploration, we aim to unravel the complexities of pollution sources, their impacts on ecosystems and human health, and the urgent call for remedial action.

Industrial Waste: The Alchemical Transformation of Water

The story of industrial waste is a tale of alchemy in reverse, where the precious resource of water is transformed into a toxic concoction. Factories and industrial plants, from textile mills to chemical manufacturers, discharge a plethora of pollutants into water bodies. Heavy metals like mercury and lead, chemicals such as PCBs (polychlorinated biphenyls), and a myriad of other substances find their way into rivers, lakes, and oceans, turning them into hazardous environments for aquatic life and human communities alike.

The impact is both immediate and insidious. In Minamata, Japan, mercury poisoning led to catastrophic health effects, a stark reminder of industrial pollution's potential to devastate. Yet, beyond these acute disasters lies a slow poisoning of ecosystems, where bioaccumulation magnifies the toxicity, moving up the food chain to eventually affect humans.

Agricultural Runoff: The Unseen Torrent

Agriculture, the backbone of human sustenance, is also a significant source of water pollution. The idyllic image of pastoral farms belies the reality of modern agriculture's reliance on synthetic fertilizers, pesticides, and herbicides. Rainfall and irrigation facilitate a silent flow of these chemicals into waterways, leading to nutrient pollution, algal blooms, and dead zones in coastal areas. The Gulf of Mexico's dead zone, an area with depleted oxygen levels, exemplifies the destructive power of nutrient runoff, suffocating marine life in its wake.

Moreover, the runoff carries sediment that clouds water bodies, disrupting aquatic plants' photosynthesis and altering habitats. The consequences ripple through ecosystems, affecting biodiversity, fish populations, and ultimately, human communities dependent on these water bodies for livelihood and sustenance.

Urban Sewage: The Civilization's Refuse

Urbanization brings with it the challenge of managing the waste of millions. Sewage, the byproduct of urban life, encompasses not only human waste but also a cocktail of pollutants from households and urban runoff, including pharmaceuticals, microplastics, and heavy metals. In many parts of the world, inadequate or nonexistent wastewater treatment facilities mean that this effluent flows directly into water bodies, contaminating them with pathogens and pollutants.

The impact on human health is profound, with waterborne diseases such as cholera and dysentery posing significant risks to communities. Moreover, the pollution undermines recreational and economic activities, affecting tourism and fisheries, and contributing to the degradation of natural beauty and biodiversity.

The Path Forward: Navigating Towards Cleaner Waters

The journey towards mitigating water pollution is fraught with challenges but not insurmountable. It requires a multifaceted approach, integrating technology, policy, and community action. Innovations in wastewater treatment, such as advanced filtration systems and bioremediation, offer hope for cleaner effluents. Policy frameworks that enforce strict regulations on pollutants, coupled with incentives for pollution reduction, can drive industries and agriculture towards more sustainable practices.

Community engagement and education play a crucial role, empowering individuals to advocate for cleaner water and adopt practices that reduce pollution at the source. Moreover, international cooperation is vital, as water pollution knows no borders, affecting shared water bodies and global oceans.

Polluted water supplies pose a grave public health crisis, disproportionately affecting the world's most vulnerable populations. The ingestion and use of contaminated water lead to a spectrum of health issues, ranging from acute illnesses to long-term chronic conditions, impacting not just individual health but also straining healthcare systems and hindering economic development. This section delves into the health implications of polluted water, emphasizing the plight of those most at risk.

Waterborne Diseases

The most immediate and visible impact of polluted water is the spread of waterborne diseases. Pathogens such as bacteria, viruses, and parasites thrive in contaminated water, leading to diseases like cholera, dysentery, hepatitis A, and typhoid fever. These illnesses are particularly rampant in areas where sewage treatment is inadequate or non-existent, and where natural water bodies serve as the primary source of drinking water. Vulnerable populations, including children, the elderly, and those with compromised immune systems, are especially susceptible to these diseases, with children under five being disproportionately affected by diarrheal diseases, one of the leading causes of child mortality globally.

Chemical Contamination

Beyond pathogens, chemical pollutants in water supplies present a more insidious threat. Heavy metals such as lead, mercury, and arsenic, along with industrial chemicals like polychlorinated biphenyls (PCBs) and pesticides, can accumulate in water sources. The consumption of chemically contaminated water can lead to a range of health issues, including neurological damage, reproductive disorders, kidney failure, and various forms of cancer. The effects of chemical exposure are often delayed, making it difficult to link them directly to polluted water, yet the long-term health implications are profound. Vulnerable populations in industrial areas or regions with intensive agriculture are particularly exposed to these risks.

Nutritional Deficiencies

Polluted water impacts not only through the presence of harmful substances but also by affecting the availability and quality of food. In agricultural communities, water pollution can degrade soil quality and contaminate crops, leading to nutritional deficiencies and food insecurity. Fish and shellfish from polluted waters may accumulate toxins, posing risks to those who rely on them as dietary staples. For populations already on the brink of malnutrition, the impact of polluted water on food sources exacerbates the cycle of poverty and disease.

Socio-economic Impacts

The health implications of polluted water extend beyond the immediate physical ailments to encompass broader socio-economic consequences. Illnesses caused by water pollution can lead to absenteeism from work or school, reducing productivity and educational attainment. The economic burden of medical treatment for water-related diseases can plunge families into poverty, while communities may face increased healthcare costs and lost economic opportunities. Vulnerable populations, lacking the resources to mitigate these impacts, bear the brunt of this cycle, perpetuating disparities in health and wealth.

Water pollution exerts a profound and often irreversible toll on ecosystems and biodiversity, disrupting the intricate balance of aquatic life and compromising the health of terrestrial habitats that depend on clean water sources. The environmental impact of water pollution extends from microscopic organisms to apex predators, affecting the entire food web and leading to long-term ecological consequences. This section explores the multifaceted environmental toll of water pollution on ecosystems and biodiversity.

Disruption of Aquatic Ecosystems

Aquatic ecosystems are particularly vulnerable to water pollution. Nutrient pollution, primarily from agricultural runoff and sewage discharge, can lead to eutrophication, a process where water bodies become overly enriched with minerals and nutrients. This leads to excessive growth of algae (algal blooms), which deplete oxygen in the water as they decompose, creating dead zones where aquatic life cannot survive. The infamous dead zone in the Gulf of Mexico, one of the largest in the world, exemplifies the devastating impact of nutrient pollution on marine ecosystems.

Heavy metals and chemical pollutants, such as mercury, lead, and industrial chemicals, can accumulate in water bodies, poisoning aquatic life. These toxins can bioaccumulate up the food chain, affecting not only the organisms that are directly exposed but also predators that consume contaminated prey.

This bioaccumulation can lead to genetic mutations, reproductive failures, and acute poisoning, drastically reducing populations of affected species.

Loss of Biodiversity

Water pollution is a significant driver of biodiversity loss in aquatic and riparian (riverbank) ecosystems. Polluted waterways can become inhospitable to endemic species, leading to declines in species diversity and abundance. Invasive species, which may be more tolerant of polluted conditions, can outcompete native species, further altering the ecological balance.

The loss of biodiversity due to water pollution has cascading effects on ecosystem services, such as water filtration, carbon sequestration, and flood regulation, which in turn affect human well-being. The decline in fish populations, for example, not only disrupts aquatic food webs but also impacts the livelihoods of communities that rely on fishing.

Impact on Terrestrial Ecosystems

The environmental toll of water pollution extends beyond aquatic environments to affect terrestrial ecosystems. Polluted water that infiltrates soil can alter its chemistry and microbiology, making it less fertile and reducing its capacity to support plant life. This can lead to decreased agricultural productivity and loss of terrestrial biodiversity as plants and animals lose their habitats and food sources.

Moreover, water pollution can affect terrestrial wildlife that depends on clean water sources. Animals that drink from polluted water bodies can suffer from the same health issues as aquatic species, including poisoning and reproductive problems, leading to declines in their populations.

The Role of Wetlands

Wetlands, which act as natural water filters, are particularly impacted by water pollution. These ecosystems are adept at removing pollutants from water through physical, chemical, and biological processes. However, when overloaded with pollutants, their capacity to purify water diminishes, leading to degraded wetland environments and the loss of their ability to provide critical ecosystem services, including acting as nurseries for a variety of species.

The Corporate Thirst

In the vast, interconnected world of global commerce and industry, corporations emerge as titans, wielding significant influence over natural resources. Among these, water—a resource as essential as air—finds itself at the heart of a complex web of usage and management, dominated by corporate interests. This chapter embarks on an exploration of the pivotal role corporations play in water usage and management, setting the stage for a deeper understanding of corporate water exploitation.

A key concept in this narrative is "virtual water"—the hidden flow of water embedded in the production and trade of goods and services. Unseen to the eye, virtual water travels the globe, embedded in agricultural products, manufactured goods, and energy sources. Its journey illuminates the vast amounts of water required to sustain global consumption patterns, often invisibly linking water-scarce regions to water-intensive products and practices. The trade and exploitation of virtual water raise critical questions about sustainability, equity, and the global distribution of water resources.

Industrial Consumption and Pollution

The Water-Intensive Nature of Various Industries

Industries such as mining, fracking, agriculture, and manufacturing stand out for their intensive water use, drawing vast quantities from the planet's finite supplies. The scale of this consumption is staggering, with implications that ripple through ecosystems, communities, and global water cycles.

- **Mining and Fracking:** These sectors are notorious for their water use, employing large volumes for extraction processes. Beyond sheer consumption, the pollution resulting from these activities—contaminated runoff, chemical spills, and groundwater infiltration—poses severe risks to surrounding water bodies.

- **Agriculture:** As the largest consumer of water globally, agriculture's thirst is unquenchable, driven by irrigation needs for crops. The sector's reliance on synthetic fertilizers and pesticides further contributes to water pollution, as runoff carries these chemicals into rivers, lakes, and groundwater.

- **Manufacturing:** The manufacturing sector's water footprint extends from cooling and processing to cleaning, with each step potentially introducing pollutants into water systems. Textile, chemical, and food processing industries are particularly water-intensive and polluting, discharging a cocktail of organic and inorganic pollutants into waterways.

Case Studies of Industrial Water Depletion and Contamination

- **The Aral Sea Disaster:** Once the fourth-largest lake in the world, the Aral Sea's demise is a stark testament to the consequences of diverting water for cotton cultivation—an agricultural practice that proved to be an ecological catastrophe, leaving behind a desert and decimated communities.

- **Fracking Operations in the United States:** The fracking boom has spotlighted the industry's vast water use and the contamination risks it poses to groundwater supplies. Instances of chemical spills and wastewater disposal have raised alarms about the long-term sustainability and health implications of this water-intensive industry.

Environmental, Social, and Health Impacts

The repercussions of industrial water consumption and pollution are far-reaching. Ecosystems are disrupted, often leading to loss of biodiversity and degradation of habitats. For communities living in proximity to industrial sites, water pollution translates into health hazards, from acute poisoning to long-term chronic conditions. Socially, the competition for water resources can exacerbate inequalities, with corporations often securing access at the expense of local needs.

Case Study 1: The Aral Sea Disaster

Background: The Aral Sea, once the fourth-largest lake in the world, straddling Kazakhstan and Uzbekistan, has become a symbol of environmental mismanagement. In the 1960s, the Soviet government initiated a project to divert the Amu Darya and Syr Darya rivers for cotton cultivation in the desert.

Water Depletion: The diversion of these rivers drastically reduced the inflow of water into the Aral Sea, causing it to shrink to less than a quarter of its original size by the early 21st century. The sea's desiccation was so severe that it split into four smaller bodies of water, with large areas becoming desert.

Contamination: The disaster also led to significant contamination. The exposed seabed, laden with pesticides and chemicals from agricultural runoff, became a source of toxic dust that was blown into surrounding communities, leading to public health crises.

Impacts: The ecological impact was devastating, with the loss of entire species of fish and birds. Economically, the local fishing industry collapsed, leading to widespread unemployment and poverty. Health issues among local populations spiked, including respiratory illnesses and cancers, attributed to the toxic dust and contaminated drinking water.

Case Study 2: Fracking Operations in the United States

Background: Hydraulic fracturing, or fracking, is a method used to extract natural gas and oil from deep underground. It involves injecting high-pressure fluid into shale rocks to release the fossil fuels. The practice has been particularly prevalent in states like Pennsylvania, Texas, and North Dakota.

Water Depletion: Fracking is water-intensive, requiring millions of gallons of water per well. This demand can strain local water resources, particularly in arid regions or during drought conditions, leading to competition with agricultural and domestic water needs.

Contamination: The process has been linked to groundwater contamination through the leakage of fracking fluids, which contain a mixture of water, sand, and chemicals, some of which are toxic. There have been instances where these chemicals have seeped into drinking water supplies, posing risks to human health.

Impacts: Beyond the immediate environmental and health risks, fracking has led to broader social and economic concerns. While it has generated significant revenue and jobs, it has also resulted in community divisions, with debates over the balance between economic benefits and environmental health. The contamination of water supplies has led to increased scrutiny and calls for stricter regulations on the industry.

Corporate Influence on Water Policy

The intricate dance between corporate interests and water policy is a complex performance, where the steps are often hidden from the public eye. Corporations, with their considerable resources and strategic interests in water usage, have developed sophisticated lobbying efforts to shape water policies and regulations to their advantage. This section delves into the mechanisms of corporate influence on water policy, highlighting the dual strategies of weakening water protection laws and securing subsidies for water use.

Lobbying for Weaker Regulations

Corporations in water-intensive industries—such as agriculture, mining, and manufacturing—often lobby for regulations that are less restrictive to their water use. This lobbying can take various forms, including direct interactions with policymakers, funding research that supports their positions, and participating in policy-making forums.

- **Example:** In the United States, agricultural lobbyists have successfully pushed for exemptions in water pollution laws, allowing for greater runoff without stringent oversight. Similarly, the fracking industry has lobbied to exclude certain chemicals used in the process from the Safe Drinking Water Act's regulations, citing proprietary concerns.

Securing Subsidies

Another facet of corporate influence is the pursuit of subsidies that reduce the cost of water usage for businesses. These subsidies can distort the true cost of water, encouraging overuse and mismanagement. Corporations often argue that such subsidies are necessary for economic growth and competitiveness, leveraging their economic contributions to secure favorable terms.

- **Example:** In many countries, agricultural subsidies include reduced rates for water use, encouraging the cultivation of water-intensive crops even in arid regions. This practice has been particularly evident in parts of the Middle East and

North Africa, where water scarcity is a pressing issue.

Campaign Contributions and the Revolving Door

Corporate influence is also exerted through campaign contributions to politicians who support their water policy positions. This financial support can sway legislative and regulatory outcomes in favor of corporate interests. Additionally, the "revolving door" phenomenon, where individuals move between roles in industry and government, can lead to conflicts of interest and policy decisions that favor corporations over public or environmental health.

International Trade Agreements

At the global level, corporations lobby for international trade agreements that include provisions affecting water rights and management. These agreements can impact local water sovereignty, allowing corporations to challenge national regulations that restrict their access to or use of water resources.

- **Example:** The inclusion of investor-state dispute settlement (ISDS) mechanisms in trade agreements has enabled corporations to sue governments over water-related regulations that they argue unfairly impact their investments, potentially undermining environmental protections and public control of water resources.

The Battle for Water Rights

The corporate influence on water policy is not without opposition. Communities, environmental groups, and some policymakers push back against efforts to weaken water protections and subsidize corporate water use. Legal battles, grassroots campaigns, and international advocacy work to counteract corporate lobbying and promote water policies that prioritize sustainability, equity, and public access.

Corporate influence in legislative processes, particularly regarding water policy, manifests through various channels, including campaign contributions to politicians and the revolving door phenomenon between industry and regulatory agencies. These mechanisms not only highlight the direct ways in which corporations seek to sway policy and regulation but also underscore the challenges in maintaining the integrity of water governance. Here are some illustrative examples:

Campaign Contributions to Politicians

United States: The agricultural and energy sectors, known for their significant water usage and pollution, are prolific contributors to political campaigns. For instance, during election cycles, these industries collectively contribute millions of dollars to candidates and political action committees (PACs) that align with their interests in loosening environmental regulations. This financial support can influence legislative priorities and the shaping of water policies that favor industry over environmental protection. A notable example includes lobbying efforts that led to exemptions for agriculture from certain provisions of the Clean Water Act, allowing for more lenient management of agricultural runoff.

The Revolving Door Between Industry and Regulatory Agencies

Global Phenomenon: The revolving door refers to the movement of individuals between roles as legislators or regulators and positions within the industries they're meant to regulate. This practice is prevalent in many countries and sectors, including water-intensive industries.

- **Example 1:** A former executive from a major oil and gas company might take up a key position in an environmental regulatory agency. Their industry background could influence regulatory decisions, potentially leading to more favorable conditions for fracking operations, including water usage and disposal practices.

- **Example 2:** In some instances, former government officials who were involved in drafting and enforcing water policies join consulting firms or legal teams representing corporations in the water sector. Their insider knowledge and connections can be leveraged to navigate regulations more effectively or to lobby for legislative changes that benefit corporate water usage.

International Trade Agreements

Impact on Local Water Sovereignty: Corporations have also influenced international trade agreements, embedding provisions that impact water rights and management. These agreements can grant corporations the power to challenge national regulations that they perceive as barriers to their operations.

- **Example:** The North American Free Trade Agreement (NAFTA) has provisions that allow companies to sue governments over regulatory changes that affect their investments, including water management practices. Cases have emerged where corporations challenge measures taken by governments to protect water resources, arguing that such measures constitute indirect expropriation of their investments.

Addressing Corporate Influence

The examples of corporate influence in legislative processes underscore the need for greater transparency, accountability, and public engagement in water policy development. Advocacy groups and civil society organizations play a crucial role in monitoring corporate influence, advocating for the public interest in water management, and pushing for reforms that ensure equitable and sustainable water governance.

International trade agreements have increasingly become a focal point for discussions on environmental governance, including the management and sovereignty of water resources. These agreements, designed primarily to facilitate trade and investment between countries, can have profound implications for local water sovereignty and management practices. The impact of such agreements on water resources is multifaceted, influencing how water is allocated, used, and conserved across borders.

Impact on Local Water Sovereignty

International trade agreements often include provisions that directly or indirectly affect water management and sovereignty. For instance:

- **Investor-State Dispute Settlement (ISDS) Mechanisms:** Many trade agreements feature ISDS mechanisms that allow investors to sue governments if policy changes or regulations negatively impact their investments. This can include measures taken to protect water resources, such as imposing stricter pollution controls or limiting water extraction rights. The threat of costly legal actions can deter governments from enacting policies that prioritize local water sovereignty and environmental protection over commercial interests.

- **Liberalization of Water Services:** Some trade agreements push for the liberalization of water services, advocating for the privatization of water supply and sanitation services. While this can lead to investments in water infrastructure, it also raises concerns about the affordability and accessibility of water for local communities, especially in developing countries where privatization may not be accompanied by sufficient regulatory oversight.

Case Studies Highlighting the Impact

- **NAFTA and Water Exports:** The North American Free Trade Agreement (NAFTA), now replaced by the United States-Mexico-Canada Agreement (USMCA), has been a subject of debate regarding water exports. Critics have argued that NAFTA could be interpreted to classify water as a tradable good, potentially opening the door for large-scale water exports from water-rich areas to water-scarce regions, undermining local water sovereignty and ecosystem sustainability.

- **The European Union's Trade Agreements:** The European Union has negotiated trade agreements that include provisions on environmental standards and water management. However, there is ongoing debate about whether these provisions are strong enough to protect local water resources and whether they effectively prevent corporations from challenging environmental regulations that impact their profits.

Challenges and Opportunities

The intersection of trade agreements and water management presents both challenges and opportunities:

- **Challenges:** Ensuring that trade agreements do not undermine local water sovereignty requires careful negotiation and robust environmental provisions. There is a risk that economic interests may overshadow environmental and social considerations, leading to policies that favor the exploitation of water resources for commercial gain.

- **Opportunities:** Trade agreements can also serve as platforms for promoting sustainable water management practices internationally. By including strong environmental clauses and mechanisms for cooperation on water conservation and protection, trade agreements can contribute to global efforts to address water scarcity and pollution.

The Battle for Water Rights

The struggle over water rights represents a critical intersection of environmental justice, corporate power, and community resilience. Around the globe, conflicts between corporations seeking to exploit water resources for profit and communities striving to protect their access to water for sustenance and cultural practices are increasingly common. These disputes often center on the allocation of water rights, where corporate interests clash with the needs of local populations and the imperative of ecological sustainability.

Corporate Encroachment on Water Sources

Corporations, particularly those in the bottled water, mining, and agriculture sectors, frequently seek access to water sources to support their operations. In some cases, governments grant these companies rights to extract water, sometimes in volumes that significantly impact the availability of water for local communities and ecosystems. This corporate encroachment can lead to situations where water, a resource that many argue should be a common good, becomes commodified, with access determined by economic power rather than community need.

Case Studies of Conflict

- **Bottling Operations in Developing Countries:** In countries like India and Pakistan, multinational beverage corporations have faced backlash for extracting groundwater for bottled water production. Communities have protested that these operations deplete local aquifers, leading to water scarcity that affects agriculture and drinking water supplies. The case of Plachimada, India, where local protests against a Coca-Cola bottling plant garnered international attention, highlights the tensions between corporate water use and community water rights.

- **Mining Operations and Water Contamination:** Mining corporations often require substantial amounts of water for their operations, leading to conflicts over water quantity and quality. In Peru, for example, mining activities have led to pollution of water sources that rural communities depend on for agriculture and daily living. Protests and legal battles have emerged as communities demand protection for their water rights and the environment.

- **Agricultural Water Rights in Drought-Prone Regions:** In regions like California's Central Valley, competition for water between agricultural corporations and local farmers intensifies during drought periods. Large agribusinesses, with their significant economic influence, often secure water rights that leave smaller farmers and rural communities struggling to access sufficient water for crops and livestock.

Legal Battles and Community-Led Resistance

The fight for water rights frequently moves to the legal arena, with communities and advocacy groups challenging corporate water use through lawsuits and regulatory appeals. These legal battles can be protracted and costly, with uncertain outcomes. However, they also serve as a crucial mechanism for asserting community rights and pushing for more equitable water governance.

Community-led resistance movements, often supported by national and international NGOs, play a pivotal role in defending water rights. Through protests, awareness campaigns, and grassroots organizing, these movements seek to hold corporations and governments accountable, advocating for policies that prioritize sustainable and equitable water use.

Towards Equitable Water Governance

The conflicts over water rights underscore the need for water governance frameworks that recognize water as a fundamental human right and a critical ecological resource. Such frameworks should ensure that community access to water is prioritized over corporate interests and that water use is managed sustainably to protect ecosystems. Key elements include:

- Participatory governance models that involve communities in decision-making about water management.

- Legal recognition of the human right to water, ensuring that all individuals have access to sufficient, safe, and affordable water.

- Regulatory mechanisms that prevent over-extraction of water resources and ensure corporate accountability for pollution and environmental degradation.

Case Study 1: Bottling Operations in India

Location: Plachimada, Kerala, India

LIQUID GOLD - THE GLOBAL CRISIS OF WATER

Conflict: The Coca-Cola Company vs. Local Community

Overview: In the early 2000s, the Coca-Cola bottling plant in Plachimada became the center of a significant conflict over water rights. The plant's operations led to the over-extraction of groundwater, resulting in a severe water shortage for the local community, which relied on the same aquifer for drinking water and agriculture.

Impact: The community reported a drastic decrease in water availability, along with pollution that rendered the remaining water unsafe for consumption or irrigation. This led to widespread protests and legal actions against the company.

Resolution: After years of legal battles and community activism, the plant was shut down in 2004. The case became a landmark in the global struggle against corporate water exploitation, highlighting the need for strict regulations on groundwater usage by corporations.

Case Study 2: Mining and Water Contamination in Peru

Location: Cajamarca, Peru

Conflict: Yanacocha Gold Mine vs. Local Farmers

Overview: The Yanacocha mine, one of the largest gold mines in the world, has faced ongoing conflicts with local communities over water use and contamination. Mining operations have been linked to pollution of local water sources with heavy metals and chemicals, affecting both human health and agriculture.

Impact: Communities reported health problems and a decline in agricultural productivity due to contaminated water. Protests and roadblocks were organized to demand action against the mine.

Resolution: The conflict has led to increased scrutiny of mining operations in Peru, with some successes in legal challenges against the mine. However, the broader issue of mining-related water contamination remains a significant challenge in the region.

Case Study 3: Agricultural Water Rights in California, USA

Location: Central Valley, California, USA

Conflict: Agribusiness vs. Small Farmers and Local Communities

Overview: California's Central Valley, a major agricultural hub, has been the site of intense competition for water, exacerbated by prolonged drought conditions. Large agribusinesses, with significant economic and political influence, often secure water rights that leave smaller farmers and local communities struggling to access water for crops and personal use.

Impact: The allocation of water rights has led to legal disputes and community activism, with small farmers and indigenous communities advocating for equitable access to water resources.

Resolution: While some progress has been made through the introduction of more sustainable water management practices and regulations, the competition for water in California remains a contentious issue, reflecting broader challenges in balancing agricultural demands with ecological sustainability and community rights.

Case Study 4: Bottling Operations in Nigeria

Location: Lagos, Nigeria

Conflict: Multinational Bottling Companies vs. Local Communities

Overview: In Nigeria, multinational bottling companies have been criticized for excessive groundwater extraction, contributing to water scarcity for local communities. The situation is compounded by pollution and inadequate infrastructure, which limit access to clean water.

Impact: Communities face difficulties in accessing sufficient clean water for daily needs, leading to reliance on expensive bottled water for drinking. This situation exacerbates economic inequalities and raises concerns about water sovereignty.

Resolution: Activism and legal challenges have emerged, aiming to hold corporations accountable and advocate for the rights of communities to access clean and affordable water. The conflict highlights the global nature of the struggle over water rights and the need for comprehensive policies to ensure equitable water access.

These case studies from India, Peru, the United States, and Nigeria illustrate the global scope of conflicts over water rights, involving a range of actors from multinational corporations to local communities. They underscore the importance of equitable water governance frameworks that prioritize human rights and ecological sustainability over corporate profits.

The global movement to protect water as a communal resource, rather than a corporate commodity, is marked by an array of legal battles and community-led resistance movements. These efforts underscore a fundamental clash between the commodification of natural resources and the rights of communities to access, manage, and protect their water sources. This analysis delves into the dynamics of these struggles, highlighting both the challenges faced by communities and the successes they have achieved in the face of corporate and sometimes governmental opposition.

Legal Battles for Water Rights

Legal battles over water rights often emerge as pivotal arenas where communities challenge the overreach of corporate interests in exploiting water resources. These legal challenges take various forms, including:

- **Litigation to Enforce Environmental Laws:** Communities and environmental organizations frequently use litigation to enforce existing environmental laws that protect water resources. For example, in the United States, the Clean Water Act has been a critical tool for communities to challenge pollution from industrial operations.

- **Challenges to Water Extraction Permits:** In many instances, communities have legally challenged the issuance of water extraction permits to corporations, arguing that such permits threaten local water supplies and ecosystems. A notable case occurred in New Zealand, where the Maori fought against water bottling companies, asserting their traditional rights to water and the need to protect it for future generations.

- **Constitutional and Human Rights Challenges:** Some communities have taken the innovative approach of framing their struggles within the broader context of constitutional and human rights. In Latin America, the concept of "Rights of Nature" has been successfully used in courts to argue against unsustainable water extraction and pollution.

Community-Led Resistance Movements

Beyond the courtroom, community-led resistance movements have been instrumental in protecting water resources. These movements often involve a combination of grassroots organizing, public awareness campaigns, direct action, and international solidarity efforts.

- **Grassroots Organizing and Direct Action:** From the Cochabamba Water War in Bolivia to the opposition against the Dakota Access Pipeline in the United States, grassroots organizing and direct action have proven effective in drawing attention to water issues and mobilizing public support. These movements often emphasize the cultural and spiritual significance of water, framing its protection as a moral imperative.

- **Public Awareness Campaigns:** Education and awareness campaigns are critical components of community-led resistance, helping to inform the public about the stakes involved in water battles and the broader implications for environmental sustainability and social justice.

- **International Solidarity:** The globalization of water issues has led to increased international solidarity among communities fighting against corporate water exploitation. Networks and coalitions, such as the Blue Planet Project, have emerged to support these local struggles, sharing resources, knowledge, and strategies across borders.

Challenges and Achievements

Communities engaged in legal battles and resistance movements face significant challenges, including disparities in resources compared to corporate entities, legal reprisals, and in some cases, violence against activists. Despite these obstacles, there have been notable successes:

- **Legal Victories:** Courts in various jurisdictions have ruled in favor of communities, setting important precedents for the protection of water resources and the rights of local populations.

- **Policy Changes:** Resistance movements have led to policy changes and the cancellation of projects that threatened water resources, demonstrating the power of collective action to effect change.

- **Increased Awareness and Solidarity:** The struggles for water rights have raised global awareness about the importance of protecting water as a communal resource, fostering a sense of solidarity and shared purpose among diverse communities.

Corporate Water Stewardship and Greenwashing

In the contemporary discourse on environmental sustainability, the concept of corporate water stewardship has emerged as a pivotal theme. It represents a commitment by companies to manage water resources responsibly and sustainably, acknowledging the finite nature of water and its critical importance to ecosystems, communities, and economies. However, the line between genuine stewardship and greenwashing—where companies portray themselves as environmentally responsible without substantiating their claims—can sometimes blur, leading to skepticism and calls for greater transparency and accountability.

Understanding Corporate Water Stewardship

Corporate water stewardship is predicated on the recognition that businesses not only impact water resources through their direct operations but also have the potential to play a significant role in addressing global water challenges. The principles of stewardship extend beyond mere compliance with regulations, advocating for proactive measures to reduce water use, protect water quality, and engage in collective actions to promote sustainable water management. This approach is often framed within the broader context of corporate social responsibility (CSR) and sustainability initiatives.

Key elements of corporate water stewardship include:

- **Water Efficiency and Reduction:** Implementing technologies and practices that reduce water consumption and improve water use efficiency in operations.

- **Pollution Prevention:** Minimizing the release of contaminants into water bodies through improved waste management and treatment processes.

- **Stakeholder Engagement:** Collaborating with local communities, governments, and NGOs to address shared water challenges and support initiatives that enhance water security and sustainability.

- **Water Risk Management:** Assessing and addressing risks related to water scarcity, quality, and regulatory changes, both within direct operations and across supply chains.

The Challenge of Greenwashing

While many companies have made genuine strides toward water stewardship, the issue of greenwashing remains a concern. Greenwashing refers to the practice of companies overstating their environmental efforts or misleading stakeholders about their environmental impact. In the context of water stewardship, greenwashing might involve publicizing water conservation projects that have minimal impact compared to the company's overall water usage or claiming sustainability credentials without independent verification.

The challenge of distinguishing genuine stewardship from greenwashing lies in the need for:

- **Transparency:** Providing clear, verifiable information about water use, impacts, and conservation efforts.

- **Third-Party Verification:** Engaging independent auditors or certification bodies to validate claims of water stewardship.

- **Holistic Approaches:** Ensuring that water stewardship efforts are part of a broader, integrated approach to environmental sustainability, rather than isolated initiatives.

Moving Beyond Greenwashing

To move beyond greenwashing, companies must embrace transparency and accountability in their water stewardship practices. This involves not only making commitments but also demonstrating progress through measurable outcomes and independent verification. Additionally, engaging stakeholders—including communities, environmental groups, and industry peers—in meaningful dialogue and collaborative efforts can enhance the credibility and impact of water stewardship initiatives.

The role of consumers, investors, and regulatory bodies in demanding and rewarding genuine stewardship cannot be understated. By prioritizing sustainability in their choices and policies, these stakeholders can incentivize companies to adopt practices that truly contribute to water conservation and sustainable management.

The increasing awareness and concern over environmental sustainability have led to the proliferation of certifications and environmental reporting mechanisms aimed at promoting responsible corporate water management. These tools are designed to provide frameworks for companies to demonstrate their commitment to sustainable practices, offering a measure of accountability and transparency in an era where water resources are under significant stress. However, the effectiveness of these mechanisms is often contingent upon the rigor of their standards, the integrity of the verification process, and the willingness of corporations to engage in meaningful environmental stewardship.

The Role of Certifications in Corporate Water Management

Certifications serve as a badge of honor for corporations, signifying adherence to specific environmental standards and practices related to water use, conservation, and management. Examples include the Alliance for Water Stewardship (AWS) Standard, which focuses on sustainable water use within a catchment context, and the ISO 14046:2014 standard on water footprint assessment, which helps organizations measure their water usage and impact.

These certifications aim to:

- **Standardize Best Practices:** By establishing clear criteria for sustainable water management, certifications help standardize what constitutes responsible water use across industries and regions.

- **Enhance Corporate Image:** Achieving certification can enhance a company's reputation, signaling to consumers, investors, and partners that it is committed to environmental sustainability.

- **Drive Improvements:** The process of obtaining certification often requires companies to assess and improve their water management practices, leading to tangible environmental benefits.

Environmental Reporting and Corporate Water Management

Environmental reporting, including disclosures related to water management, allows companies to communicate their environmental performance and sustainability efforts to stakeholders. Frameworks such as the Global Reporting Initiative (GRI) and the Carbon Disclosure Project (CDP) provide guidelines for reporting on water usage, risks, and conservation measures.

The benefits of environmental reporting include:

- **Transparency:** Reporting offers a window into a company's environmental impact, including its water management practices, fostering transparency and accountability.

- **Benchmarking and Improvement:** Through reporting, companies can benchmark their performance against peers and identify areas for improvement in their water management strategies.

- **Stakeholder Engagement:** Effective reporting engages a range of stakeholders, from investors to consumers, informing them of the company's sustainability efforts and challenges.

Challenges in Verifying and Enforcing Sustainable Practices

Despite the potential benefits of certifications and environmental reporting, several challenges persist in verifying and enforcing sustainable water management practices:

- **Variability in Standards:** The variability in certification standards and the rigor of environmental reporting guidelines can lead to inconsistencies in how water sustainability is measured and reported.

- **Greenwashing Risks:** There is a risk that certifications and environmental reports can be used as tools for greenwashing, where companies exaggerate their commitment to sustainability without making significant environmental improvements.

- **Verification and Enforcement:** Ensuring the accuracy of self-reported data and the integrity of certification processes requires robust verification mechanisms. However, the capacity for enforcing these standards and holding companies accountable for misleading claims or non-compliance can be limited.

- **Complexity of Water Issues:** Water issues are often highly localized and context-specific, making it challenging to apply uniform standards across different regions and industries. This complexity can complicate the assessment of a company's water footprint and the effectiveness of its management practices.

Moving Forward

To enhance the role of certifications and environmental reporting in promoting sustainable corporate water management, several steps can be taken:

- **Strengthening Standards and Verification Processes:** Developing more rigorous and universally accepted standards, along with robust third-party verification processes, can help ensure that certifications and reports accurately reflect a company's water management practices.

- **Enhancing Transparency and Stakeholder Engagement:** Encouraging greater transparency in environmental reporting and more meaningful engagement with stakeholders can help build trust and facilitate collaborative efforts to address water sustainability challenges.

- **Focusing on Impact:** Shifting the focus from mere compliance to the actual environmental impact of water management practices can encourage companies to adopt more meaningful and effective sustainability measures.

LIQUID GOLD - THE GLOBAL CRISIS OF WATER

Towards Equitable Water Governance

The quest for equitable water governance seeks to reconcile the often competing demands of sustainability, equity, community access, and economic development. In the face of growing water scarcity and pollution, exacerbated by climate change and industrial expansion, the traditional models of water governance—frequently characterized by top-down management and corporate influence—increasingly fall short. This exploration delves into alternative models that prioritize the communal and ecological value of water, offering pathways to a more sustainable and just water future.

Community-Based Water Management

Community-based water management (CBWM) represents a paradigm shift towards local stewardship of water resources. This model emphasizes the involvement of local communities in the decision-making processes regarding water use, conservation, and management. CBWM initiatives often incorporate traditional knowledge and practices, which can offer sustainable solutions adapted to local environmental conditions.

- **Benefits:** CBWM can lead to more equitable water distribution, as community needs and priorities directly inform management decisions. Additionally, by fostering a sense of ownership and responsibility towards local water sources, CBWM can enhance community engagement in conservation efforts.

- **Challenges:** Implementing CBWM requires overcoming institutional barriers and shifting power dynamics, particularly in regions where water resources have been heavily privatized or are under central government control.

Integrated Water Resources Management (IWRM)

IWRM advocates for the coordinated development and management of water, land, and related resources to maximize economic and social welfare without compromising the sustainability of vital ecosystems. This approach recognizes the interconnectedness of water with broader environmental and societal factors.

- **Benefits:** IWRM can address the multifaceted challenges of water governance by promoting cross-sectoral collaboration, balancing competing water uses, and integrating environmental conservation into water management practices.

- **Challenges:** Effective implementation of IWRM requires strong institutional frameworks, inter-sectoral coordination, and the harmonization of policies across different levels of governance.

Public-Private Partnerships (PPPs)

While the involvement of private entities in water management has been contentious, carefully structured public-private partnerships (PPPs) can offer a model for leveraging the strengths of both sectors. The key is ensuring that such partnerships are designed with clear accountability mechanisms, equitable risk-sharing, and a strong focus on public benefit.

- **Benefits:** PPPs can mobilize additional resources for water infrastructure and innovation, potentially improving efficiency and service delivery.

- **Challenges:** To avoid the pitfalls of privatization, PPPs must include safeguards to protect community access to water, maintain affordable pricing, and ensure sustainable water use practices.

Rights-Based Approaches

Rights-based approaches to water governance emphasize the recognition of water as a fundamental human right. This perspective advocates for legal frameworks that guarantee access to safe and sufficient water for all individuals, prioritizing human and ecological needs over commercial interests.

- **Benefits:** A rights-based approach can strengthen legal protections for water access, provide a framework for addressing inequalities, and empower communities to claim their water rights.

- **Challenges:** Implementing rights-based approaches requires political will, legal reforms, and the development of mechanisms to enforce water rights effectively.

Towards Equitable Water Governance

The quest for equitable water governance seeks to balance the scales between corporate interests and the fundamental human right to water. It emphasizes sustainability, equity, and community access, challenging the traditional paradigms that have often prioritized profit over people and the environment. This section explores alternative models for water governance through case studies that highlight successful community management of water resources and innovative public-private partnerships (PPPs) that have fostered improved water sustainability and access.

Case Study 1: Community-Led Water Management in Rajasthan, India

Background: In the semi-arid region of Rajasthan, India, traditional water harvesting structures, known as "johads," had fallen into disrepair, leading to water scarcity and agricultural decline. The NGO Tarun Bharat Sangh, led by Rajendra Singh, initiated a grassroots movement to revive these ancient systems.

Model: The initiative was community-led, involving local villagers in the restoration of johads. This effort not only revived traditional knowledge but also fostered a sense of ownership and responsibility towards water resources among the community members.

Impact: The restoration of over 10,000 johads across Rajasthan transformed the landscape, replenishing groundwater levels, reviving rivers that had been dry for decades, and significantly improving agricultural productivity. This success story, often referred to as the "water revolution," highlights the potential of community-led water management to achieve sustainable water access and enhance resilience to drought.

Case Study 2: Public-Private Partnership for Water Access in Manila, Philippines

Background: Manila, the capital of the Philippines, faced significant challenges in providing access to clean water for its growing population. In 1997, the city's water supply system was privatized in an effort to improve efficiency and expand access, resulting in two major PPPs.

Model: The PPPs involved the concession of the city's water supply system to two private companies, Manila Water Company and Maynilad Water Services, under strict regulatory oversight to ensure service quality and fair pricing. The agreements included targets for expanding access to underserved areas and investments in infrastructure.

Impact: The PPP model in Manila led to substantial improvements in water access and quality for millions of residents. Manila Water Company, in particular, was successful in expanding service coverage from 67% in 1997 to over 93% by the mid-2010s, significantly reducing waterborne diseases and improving public health outcomes. The Manila case demonstrates the potential of well-structured PPPs to enhance water access and sustainability, provided that there is effective regulatory oversight and a commitment to serving the public interest.

Case Study 3: Participatory Irrigation Management in Brazil

Background: In the semi-arid region of Northeast Brazil, smallholder farmers faced challenges in accessing reliable water sources for irrigation. The government-initiated a participatory irrigation management program to empower local farmer associations to manage and maintain irrigation schemes.

Model: The model was based on the formation of local water user associations, which were given control over the operation and maintenance of irrigation infrastructure. This participatory approach encouraged collective decision-making and resource sharing among farmers.

Impact: The program led to improved water efficiency, increased agricultural productivity, and higher incomes for smallholder farmers. By involving farmers directly in water management, the initiative fostered sustainable irrigation practices and strengthened community resilience against drought.

The increasing pressures on global water resources from population growth, industrialization, and climate change underscore the urgent need for comprehensive policies and international frameworks that ensure equitable water distribution and recognize water as a global commons. Addressing these challenges requires a multifaceted approach, integrating local needs and global priorities, to foster sustainable water management practices that benefit all. Here, we discuss policy recommendations and explore international frameworks that aim to achieve these goals.

Policy Recommendations

Implement Integrated Water Resources Management (IWRM)

IWRM promotes the coordinated development and management of water, land, and related resources to maximize economic and social welfare without compromising the sustainability of vital ecosystems. Policies should encourage the adoption of IWRM principles at all levels of governance, emphasizing cross-sectoral collaboration, stakeholder participation, and the balancing of diverse water uses with environmental protection.

Strengthen Water Governance Structures

Effective water governance is crucial for equitable water distribution. Policies should aim to strengthen governance structures by enhancing transparency, accountability, and public participation in water management decisions. This includes establishing clear legal frameworks for water rights, promoting community-based management practices, and ensuring that governance mechanisms are inclusive and equitable.

Prioritize Water Conservation and Efficiency

With the growing demand for water, conservation and efficiency are paramount. Policies should incentivize the adoption of water-saving technologies, the development of drought-resistant crop varieties, and the implementation of water reuse and recycling practices. Public awareness campaigns can also play a significant role in promoting water conservation at the individual and community levels.

Protect and Restore Ecosystems

Ecosystems play a critical role in maintaining the water cycle and ensuring water quality. Policies should prioritize the protection and restoration of wetlands, rivers, lakes, and forests, which act as natural water infrastructure. This includes implementing measures to reduce pollution, prevent habitat destruction, and mitigate the impacts of climate change on water resources.

International Frameworks

The Sustainable Development Goals (SDGs)

The United Nations' SDGs, particularly Goal 6, which aims to "ensure availability and sustainable management of water and sanitation for all," provide a comprehensive framework for addressing global water challenges. Policies should align with the targets set under SDG 6, focusing on improving water quality, increasing water-use efficiency, and supporting the participation of local communities in water management.

The Dublin Principles

The Dublin Statement on Water and Sustainable Development, adopted at the 1992 International Conference on Water and the Environment, outlines four guiding principles for water management, including the recognition of water as an economic good and the importance of participatory decision-making. Policies should reflect these principles, emphasizing the value of water and the need for inclusive governance approaches.

The Human Right to Water

In 2010, the United Nations General Assembly recognized the human right to safe and clean drinking water and sanitation. Policies should ensure that this right is upheld, prioritizing access to water for the most vulnerable populations and integrating human rights considerations into water governance frameworks.

Conclusion

Ah, we've navigated the vast and sometimes turbulent waters of corporate water use and governance, haven't we? Like a ship making its way through the Sargasso Sea, we've encountered areas dense with the seaweed of complexity and the occasional vortex of corporate interests. Yet, here we are, approaching the harbor with our cargo of insights, ready for the unloading.

In this journey, we've seen that water, much like the universe, is vast, mysterious, and essential for life. Yet, unlike the cosmos, where stars are born and die over millennia, our water resources are under immediate threat, squeezed by the gravitational forces of corporate exploitation. It's clear that a paradigm shift is needed—a shift in how we value and manage this life-sustaining resource, akin to realizing that Earth is not the center of the universe but merely a speck in the infinite cosmic dance.

Our call to action, then, is not just a whisper into the void. It's a clarion call to policymakers, activists, and consumers to advocate for responsible water use, to champion initiatives that place the human right to water above the insatiable thirst for profits. It's a reminder that, in the grand scheme of things, ensuring access to clean water for all is a reflection of our humanity, our capacity for empathy, and our ability to prioritize the collective good over individual gain.

The potential for collective action and international cooperation to address the challenges posed by corporate control of water resources is immense. Like particles entangled across vast distances, our actions here can have ripple effects far beyond our immediate surroundings. By coming together, sharing knowledge, and pushing for change, we can create a wave of momentum towards better water stewardship—a wave so powerful it reshapes the landscape of water governance.

As we conclude this chapter, let's reflect on the journey we've undertaken. We've explored the depths of corporate water exploitation and glimpsed the possibilities for a more sustainable and equitable water future. This exploration is not just an academic exercise; it's a roadmap for action, a guide to navigating the complex interplay between water resources and corporate interests.

In the end, the story of water on our planet is still being written. And while the challenges are significant, the opportunities for positive change are boundless. Together, through informed action and unwavering commitment, we can ensure that water—our most precious resource—remains a source of life and sustenance for all, not a commodity to be hoarded and exploited. Let's set sail towards that future, shall we? After all, the universe may be infinite, but our supply of water is not. Let's treat it with the care and reverence it deserves.

Liquid Resistance

Liquid Resistance

In a world where the ripples of water privatization and pollution spread far and wide, touching the shores of distant lands and the hearts of diverse communities, a wave of resistance and activism has risen. This chapter, "Liquid Resistance," dives into the real stories of individuals and communities who have stood up against the tide of corporate control over water resources, weaving a tapestry of hope, resilience, and collective action.

The Essence of Resistance

At the heart of every resistance story is a simple truth: water is life. From the bustling streets of megacities to the quiet pathways of rural villages, the fight against water privatization and pollution is driven by a deep-seated belief in water as a communal right, not a commodity to be bought and sold. It's a narrative that resonates with the soulful humor of shared human experiences and the astute observation that, in the grand cosmos of existence, ensuring access to clean water is a reflection of our values and priorities as a civilization.

Stories from the Frontlines

- **The Cochabamba Water War:** In Bolivia, the people of Cochabamba took to the streets in the early 2000s, in a David-versus-Goliath battle against a multinational corporation that had taken control of their water supply. Their victory, a testament to the power of grassroots mobilization, not only reclaimed their water but also sparked a global conversation about water rights.

• **The Guardians of the Great Lakes:** In North America, indigenous communities and environmental activists have formed a formidable alliance to protect the Great Lakes from pollution and unsustainable extraction. Their efforts underscore the importance of honoring traditional knowledge and the interconnectedness of all life.

• **The Green Walk for Water:** Across the plains of Africa, communities have embarked on long walks to draw attention to the water crisis, turning each step into a statement against water privatization and for the sustainable management of water resources. These walks, a blend of protest and pilgrimage, highlight the resilience of the human spirit in the face of adversity.

The Fight for the Ganges, India

Background: The Ganges River, considered sacred by millions, has faced severe pollution from industrial waste, sewage, and religious offerings. The "Save Ganga Movement" is a widespread environmental initiative involving activists, spiritual leaders, and local communities advocating for the river's cleanup and protection.

Resistance: Activists like GD Agarwal undertook hunger strikes to pressure the government into taking concrete actions to protect the Ganges. Public campaigns and legal actions by environmental groups have led to the establishment of the National Ganga River Basin Authority and efforts to enforce stricter pollution control measures.

Standing Rock Sioux Tribe, USA

Background: The Dakota Access Pipeline (DAPL) protests, led by the Standing Rock Sioux Tribe in North Dakota, became a global symbol of indigenous rights and environmental activism. The tribe opposed the pipeline's construction, fearing it would pollute the Missouri River, their primary water source, and desecrate sacred lands.

Resistance: Thousands of activists, including indigenous peoples from across the globe, environmentalists, and veterans, gathered at the Standing Rock reservation to protest the pipeline. Despite facing harsh weather conditions and confrontations with law enforcement, the movement drew international attention to the issues of indigenous sovereignty and environmental justice.

The El Zapotillo Dam Controversy, Mexico

Background: The construction of the El Zapotillo Dam on the Verde River in Jalisco was intended to supply water to

Guadalajara but threatened to submerge several communities, including Temacapulín, Acasico, and Palmarejo, displacing hundreds of residents.

Resistance: The affected communities banded together to form the "Salvemos Temacapulín, Acasico y Palmarejo" movement, organizing protests, legal challenges, and awareness campaigns. Their persistent efforts have delayed the project and brought national attention to the human rights issues surrounding large-scale water projects.

The Anti-Privatization Struggle in Jakarta, Indonesia

Background: Jakarta's water supply system was privatized in the late 1990s, leading to increased tariffs, poor service quality, and unequal access to clean water. The city's residents faced frequent water shortages and high prices.

Resistance: A coalition of residents, activists, and NGOs launched a legal challenge against the privatization, arguing that it violated the right to water. In 2015, the Jakarta Central District Court ruled in favor of the plaintiffs, marking a significant victory against water privatization. The decision was hailed as a landmark case for water rights activists worldwide.

The Water Crisis in Flint, Michigan, USA

Background: The city of Flint faced a public health crisis when its drinking water became contaminated with lead after the city switched its water source to the Flint River without adequate treatment.

Resistance: Residents, supported by activists and researchers, mobilized to demand action from local and state officials. Their persistence led to widespread media coverage, congressional hearings, and the eventual return to a safer water source. The Flint water crisis remains a poignant reminder of the importance of vigilant and responsive water management.

The Anti-Dam Movements in Brazil

Background: Brazil has seen significant opposition to hydroelectric dam projects in the Amazon basin, which threaten indigenous lands, biodiversity, and the livelihoods of local communities. The Belo Monte Dam, one of the world's largest hydroelectric projects, has been a focal point of these protests.

Resistance: Indigenous groups, environmental activists, and local residents have organized protests, legal challenges, and international campaigns to highlight the social and environmental impacts of the dam. Their efforts have brought global attention to the issue, although the dam was eventually constructed, sparking ongoing debates about energy policy and indigenous rights in Brazil.

The Water Defenders of El Salvador

Background: In El Salvador, a small Central American country facing severe water stress, communities fought against mining operations that threatened their water sources. The proposed El Dorado mine was a particular point of contention due to concerns over water contamination and depletion.

Resistance: A coalition of community organizations, environmental groups, and the Catholic Church launched a decade-long campaign against metal mining in the country, citing the risks to the nation's water supply. Their efforts culminated in a historic victory in 2017 when El Salvador became the first country in the world to ban metal mining outright, prioritizing water security over mining profits.

The Sardar Sarovar Dam Protests in India

Background: The construction of the Sardar Sarovar Dam on the Narmada River in India was met with widespread protests due to its environmental impact and the displacement of thousands of families.

Resistance: The Narmada Bachao Andolan (Save the Narmada Movement), led by activist Medha Patkar, mobilized affected communities and garnered international support for their cause. The movement highlighted issues of environmental justice, sustainable development, and the rights of indigenous peoples, leading to partial success in terms of compensation and rehabilitation measures for displaced communities.

The Fight for the Right to Water in Detroit, USA

Background: Detroit, Michigan, faced a water crisis when the city began shutting off water to thousands of households over unpaid bills, disproportionately affecting low-income and minority communities.

Resistance: Grassroots groups, activists, and residents organized protests, legal actions, and water distribution networks to assist affected families. The United Nations condemned the water shutoffs as a violation of human rights, and the activism in Detroit sparked a broader national conversation about water affordability and the human right to water.

The Vittel Controversy in France

- **Nestlé's Water Extraction:** Local opposition against Nestlé for over-extracting groundwater in Vittel, leading to concerns about future water scarcity for residents.

The Anti-Privatization Protests in Greece

- **Fighting Water Privatization:** Widespread protests against the proposed privatization of public water utilities in Athens and Thessaloniki, emphasizing water as a human right.

The Save the Conwy River Campaign, UK

- **Hydroelectric Development Opposition:** Activists and local communities opposed a hydroelectric scheme on the Conwy River in Wales, citing environmental and recreational impacts.

The Klamath River Dam Removal, USA

- **Largest Dam Removal Project:** A coalition of Native American tribes, environmentalists, and fishermen advocated for the removal of four dams on the Klamath River to restore salmon habitats.

The Berlin Water Referendum, Germany

- **Re-municipalization of Water Services:** Citizens in Berlin successfully campaigned for a referendum that led to the city buying back control of its water services from private companies.

The Anti-Fracking Movement in Algeria

- **Opposition to Shale Gas Fracking:** Protests erupted across Algeria against government plans to explore and exploit shale gas, citing water use and pollution concerns.

The Water Is Life Movement in New Zealand

- **Maori Opposition to Water Bottling:** Maori communities opposed water bottling companies given rights to extract groundwater, emphasizing the cultural and ecological significance of water.

LIQUID GOLD - THE GLOBAL CRISIS OF WATER

The March for Water in South Africa

- **Protesting Water Mismanagement:** Communities marched in Cape Town and other cities against water mismanagement and inequality in access, amid a severe drought.

The Power of Collective Action

The stories of liquid resistance are as diverse as the ecosystems that water sustains, yet they share a common thread: the belief in collective action. When communities come together, their combined strength can challenge the status quo, pushing for policies that prioritize the human right to water over corporate profits. This collective action, a symphony of voices from different corners of the globe, is a powerful force for change, demonstrating that when it comes to protecting our most precious resource, unity is our greatest strength.

Towards a Sustainable and Equitable Water Future

As we navigate the currents of the 21st century, the need for a paradigm shift in how water is valued and managed becomes increasingly clear. The stories of liquid resistance offer valuable lessons in the power of community, the importance of stewardship, and the potential for change. They call on policymakers, activists, and consumers to advocate for responsible water use and to support initiatives that ensure water remains a right for all, not a privilege for the few.

In the face of corporate exploitation of water resources, the global movement towards better water stewardship is gaining momentum. It's a movement fueled by the conviction that water is a shared heritage, a connector of lives and cultures, and a critical component of our collective well-being on this blue planet we call home.

The role of technology and innovation in addressing water scarcity and pollution

The role of technology and innovation in addressing water scarcity and pollution is pivotal, offering a beacon of hope in the quest for sustainable water management. As the world grapples with the dual challenges of ensuring adequate water supply for a growing population and protecting water bodies from pollution, technological advancements and innovative approaches emerge as key tools in the arsenal against these pressing issues. Here's an overview of how technology and innovation are making strides in tackling water scarcity and pollution:

Advancements in Water Treatment Technologies

- **Desalination:** Innovations in desalination, such as reverse osmosis and forward osmosis, are making it more energy-efficient and cost-effective to convert seawater into potable water. This technology is particularly crucial for arid regions with limited freshwater resources.

- **Wastewater Recycling:** Advanced treatment processes, including membrane bioreactors (MBRs) and ultraviolet (UV) disinfection, enable the safe reuse of wastewater for agricultural, industrial, and even potable purposes, significantly reducing the demand on freshwater sources.

Smart Water Management Systems

- **Internet of Things (IoT) and AI:** IoT devices and artificial intelligence (AI) are revolutionizing water management by enabling real-time monitoring and analysis of water use, quality, and infrastructure integrity. These technologies facilitate leak detection, predictive maintenance, and efficient water distribution, minimizing losses and optimizing usage.

- **Remote Sensing and GIS:** Geographic Information Systems (GIS) and remote sensing technologies offer powerful tools for mapping water resources, monitoring changes in water bodies, and identifying pollution sources. This data is invaluable for informed decision-making and targeted intervention strategies.

Pollution Control and Cleanup Innovations

- **Bioremediation:** Leveraging natural processes, bioremediation uses microorganisms or plants to detoxify polluted water bodies. This eco-friendly approach is effective for treating a range of pollutants, including heavy metals and organic contaminants.

• **Nanotechnology:** Nanomaterials, with their high surface area and reactivity, are being explored for water purification applications. They offer potential for efficiently removing pollutants, pathogens, and even salt from water.

Water-Efficient Agricultural Practices

• **Precision Agriculture:** Technologies like drip irrigation and soil moisture sensors allow for precise water application in agriculture, significantly reducing water use while maintaining crop yields. Coupled with data analytics, these tools help farmers make informed decisions about irrigation, optimizing water use.

Community-Driven and Open-Source Innovations

• **Decentralized Solutions:** Grassroots innovations, including rainwater harvesting systems and community-managed purification units, empower local communities to address their water challenges directly. Open-source technologies and knowledge sharing platforms facilitate the dissemination of these low-cost, scalable solutions.

Challenges and Opportunities

While technology and innovation offer promising pathways to address water scarcity and pollution, their deployment faces challenges, including high costs, maintenance requirements, and the need for technical expertise. Moreover, ensuring equitable access to these technologies remains a significant concern, particularly in developing regions.

A Drop in the Bucket: Solutions for a Thirsty World

A Drop in the Bucket: Solutions for a Thirsty World

The global water crisis presents one of the most formidable challenges of the 21st century, threatening ecosystems, human health, and economic development across the globe. Yet, within this crisis lies an opportunity for innovation, technology, and collective action to forge a sustainable path forward. Here, we explore a spectrum of solutions, from traditional practices like conservation and rainwater harvesting to advanced technologies such as desalination and wastewater recycling, each holding a promise to mitigate water scarcity and pollution.

Water Conservation and Efficiency

Key Strategy: Reducing water usage through conservation and improving water use efficiency in agriculture, industry, and domestic settings.

Approaches:

- **Smart Irrigation Systems:** Utilizing soil moisture sensors and weather forecasts to optimize irrigation schedules and reduce water waste in agriculture.

- **Low-Flow Fixtures:** Installing water-efficient toilets, showerheads, and faucets in homes and businesses to cut down on unnecessary water consumption.

Rainwater Harvesting

Key Strategy: Capturing and storing rainwater for reuse, reducing dependence on groundwater and surface water sources.

Approaches:

- **Rooftop Harvesting Systems:** Collecting rainwater from roofs and storing it in tanks for irrigation, flushing toilets, and even potable uses after proper treatment.

- **Permeable Pavements:** Using porous materials for pavements to enhance the recharge of groundwater and reduce urban runoff.

Desalination

Key Strategy: Converting seawater or brackish water into fresh water, addressing water scarcity in coastal and arid regions.

Approaches:

- **Reverse Osmosis:** Employing semi-permeable membranes to remove salts and impurities from seawater, though energy-intensive, is becoming more efficient with advances in technology.

- **Solar Desalination:** Harnessing solar energy to evaporate water, leaving salts behind, and condensing the vapor into fresh water, offering a sustainable alternative.

Wastewater Recycling and Reuse

Key Strategy: Treating and reusing wastewater for agricultural, industrial, and even potable purposes, significantly reducing the demand for fresh water.

Approaches:

- **Advanced Treatment Technologies:** Using membrane bioreactors, ultraviolet disinfection, and other technologies to purify wastewater to high standards.

- **Greywater Systems:** Separating and treating lightly contaminated water from showers, sinks, and laundry for reuse in irrigation and toilet flushing.

Nature-Based Solutions

Key Strategy: Leveraging natural processes and ecosystems to improve water quality and availability.

Approaches:

- **Constructed Wetlands:** Creating wetlands to treat wastewater through natural filtration processes, enhancing biodiversity while purifying water.

- **Riparian Buffers:** Planting vegetation along waterways to filter pollutants from runoff, stabilize banks, and improve habitat quality.

Policy and Community Engagement

Key Strategy: Developing policies that promote sustainable water management and engaging communities in water conservation efforts.

Approaches:

- **Water Pricing:** Implementing pricing strategies that reflect the true cost of water, encouraging conservation and investment in efficient technologies.

- **Education and Awareness:** Raising awareness about water issues and promoting water-saving behaviors through education campaigns and community-based projects.

International cooperation and policy reform in managing global water resources – it's a bit like trying to organize a family dinner where everyone's a picky eater, and you've only got tofu and kale on the menu. Everyone knows it's good for them, but getting everyone to happily dig in is another story entirely.

Now, imagine the world's water resources as a giant, communal pot of soup. It's the only pot we've got, and we're all huddled around it with our spoons at the ready. The thing is, some folks have brought ladles to this spoon party, and others are trying to sip with teaspoons that have seen better days. It's clear we need some ground rules, or else we'll end up with a scorched pot and a lot of hungry, disgruntled diners.

The Recipe for Disaster (Or, How Not to Manage Global Water Resources)

First, let's talk about the chefs in this kitchen – the policymakers and international bodies. They're trying to season this soup to everyone's taste, but there's a catch. Not everyone agrees on the recipe. Some are all in for a spicy broth, heavy on industrial growth and economic spices, while others are advocating for a more organic blend, focusing on sustainability and conservation herbs.

And then there's the issue of who gets to stir the pot. Countries with the biggest ladles (read: economic power) often end up doing most of the stirring, leaving smaller, teaspoon-wielding nations to hope they get a fair taste. It's a classic case of too many cooks in the kitchen, except some cooks have been relegated to dishwashing duties against their will.

A Pinch of International Cooperation

What we need is a bit of international cooperation – a way for all the cooks to agree on a recipe that keeps the soup nutritious and plentiful for everyone. This means setting aside those ladles and teaspoons and agreeing on a uniform spoon size. Easier said than done, right? It's like trying to convince everyone at a rock concert to sing in harmony; it's a beautiful idea but good luck orchestrating it.

A Dash of Policy Reform

Policy reform is the secret sauce to making this communal soup a sustainable feast. It's about agreeing to use ingredients that replenish the pot rather than deplete it. Think renewable water sources, conservation techniques, and pollution control measures. But here's the kicker: everyone's got to be willing to tweak their family recipes. This means big ladle countries might have to tone down the industrial seasoning, and teaspoon nations might need support to grow their own sustainable herbs.

The Perfect Blend

Achieving the perfect blend of international cooperation and policy reform is akin to baking a soufflé. It requires precision, patience, and a bit of magic. It's about finding that sweet spot where economic development doesn't come at the expense of our planet's most precious resource: water.

So, as we stand around this metaphorical pot of soup, let's remember that we're all in this kitchen together. It's time to roll up our sleeves, agree on a recipe, and ensure that our global water resources are managed in a way that leaves no one hungry. After all, a well-fed world is a happy world, and who doesn't want to be part of making that a reality?

Ah, a sustainable water future – it's like envisioning a world where unicorns prance through lush, verdant meadows, and chocolate doesn't have calories. A beautiful thought, indeed, but as we stand ankle-deep in the muddied waters of reality, such a vision seems as distant as a mirage in the desert. Yet, let's indulge in a bit of hopeful stoicism, shall we? After all, if humanity can invent smartphones and send people to space, surely we can figure out how to manage a bit of H2O.

Equitable Access: A Pipe Dream?

Imagine a world where water doesn't discriminate – a utopia where it flows freely, not just through the golden faucets of the affluent but into the humble cups of the impoverished. Equitable access to water, a notion as radical as expecting cats to finally acknowledge their domestication. Yet, here lies the cornerstone of our vision. By embracing the radical idea that water is a right, not a privilege, we embark on the first step towards a future where thirst is merely a signal to drink, not a desperate plea for survival.

Efficient Use: The Art of Not Pouring Water Down the Drain

Efficiency in water use – now, there's a concept. In a world where leaving the tap running while brushing your teeth is seen as a cardinal sin, we find the essence of conservation. It's about treating every drop of water like a precious gem, not because we're miserly, but because we're wise. We innovate, we recycle, and we treat wastewater until it's fit for a king. The goal? To ensure that our children look at us bewildered when we tell tales of water wastage, as if we were spinning yarns of a time when people smoked on airplanes.

Environmental Stewardship: Becoming Nature's Best Friend

And then, we have environmental stewardship – the act of treating the planet like a cherished garden rather than a disposable playground. It's a commitment to leaving a place better than we found it, ensuring that rivers, lakes, and oceans aren't just receptacles for our refuse. This part of the vision involves a handshake with nature, a promise to protect its cycles and habitats as if our lives depended on it – because, well, they do.

The Stoic's Path to Water Utopia

So, how do we march stoically towards this vision, with cynicism as our shield and hope as our spear? It begins with a collective shrug at the enormity of the task, followed by a determined step forward. We innovate not just technologically but socially, crafting policies that reflect our shared humanity and environmental reality. We educate, turning every man, woman, and child into a steward of the earth. And most importantly, we collaborate, because the future of water is a puzzle that requires every piece, from every corner of the globe, to complete.

In this vision of a sustainable water future, we find a challenge to our ingenuity, our compassion, and our ability to act as one. It's a vision that demands we rise above our baser instincts to squabble and hoard, and instead, extend a hand – both to our neighbor and to the natural world. After all, if we're to dream, let's dream of a world where water – the source of all life – becomes the wellspring of our greatest achievements.

100 facts (not so known) about Water

1. **Ancient Water:** Some of the water on Earth is older than the sun, having originated in the cold, ancient molecular clouds in the galaxy.
2. **Walking Water:** The Australian water-holding frog can store up to half its body weight in water and "walk" it across the land, distributing it during dry periods.
3. **Fog Harvesting:** Communities in arid regions, like parts of Chile, use large mesh nets to harvest fog, collecting water droplets from the air as a source of fresh water.
4. **Biological Water Filter:** The roots of the water hyacinth, an aquatic plant, can naturally filter and purify water, removing pollutants and heavy metals.
5. **Ice Worms:** There are species of worms, known as ice worms, that can live entirely within glacier ice, surviving in temperatures that would freeze most life forms.
6. **Underwater Lakes and Rivers:** In places like the Black Sea and the Gulf of Mexico, underwater lakes and rivers complete with banks and waves have been discovered, formed by differences in salinity.
7. **The Boiling River:** In the Amazon, there's a river so hot that it boils. The water reaches temperatures up to 93°C (200°F) due to geothermal heating.
8. **Water in Space:** Water is not only found on Earth;

vast amounts of water exist in space, including on Mars, in the atmospheres of giant planets, and in the form of ice on comets and moons.

9. **Transpiration:** A large oak tree can transpire 40,000 gallons of water into the atmosphere each year, essentially "breathing" out water vapor through its leaves.

10. **Water's Anomaly:** Water is one of the few substances that expand when it freezes, making ice less dense than liquid water, which is why ice floats.

11. **The Mpemba Effect:** Hot water can sometimes freeze faster than cold water, a phenomenon known as the Mpemba effect, which still puzzles scientists.

12. **Atmospheric Rivers:** Long, narrow regions in the atmosphere can transport water vapor roughly equivalent to the average flow of water at the mouth of the Mississippi River.

13. **Living Stones:** The Lithops, a succulent plant, can store water in its leaves, allowing it to survive in arid environments by mimicking the appearance of stones.

14. **Water Footprint of Products:** It takes about 2,700 liters (713 gallons) of water to produce one cotton shirt, highlighting the concept of "virtual water" used in goods production.

15. **Photic Zone:** In the ocean, the photic zone, where sunlight penetrates the water, rarely extends deeper than 200 meters (656 feet), leaving the vast majority of the world's oceans in perpetual darkness.

16. **The Color of Water:** Pure water has a slight blue

tint, which becomes noticeable in large quantities due to the absorption and scattering of light.

17. **Water and Electricity:** Water is an excellent conductor of electricity due to dissolved salts and minerals, which is why it's dangerous to mix water and electricity.

18. **Thermal Properties:** Water has a high specific heat capacity, meaning it can absorb a lot of heat before it begins to get hot, playing a crucial role in Earth's climate.

19. **Water Memory Myth:** Despite popular claims, scientific evidence does not support the idea that water has memory or that it can be structurally altered by emotional or energetic influences.

20. **Rare Natural Phenomenon:** Under specific conditions, water can simultaneously exist in its three states: solid, liquid, and gas, in a natural phenomenon known as the triple point.

21. **Aquatic Plants' Oxygen Production:** Aquatic plants produce a significant portion of the world's oxygen through photosynthesis, much of it underwater.

22. **Deepest Point in the Ocean:** The Challenger Deep in the Mariana Trench is the deepest known point in the Earth's seabed, with pressures over 1,000 times the standard atmospheric pressure at sea level, yet it still contains water.

23. **Water's Role in Plate Tectonics:** Water acts as a lubricant for the movement of tectonic plates. Subducted water lowers the melting point of rocks,

facilitating magma formation and volcanic activity.

24. **Ancient Water Storage:** The qanat system, developed in ancient Persia over 3,000 years ago for irrigation, is an early example of sustainable water management, some of which are still in use today.

25. **Water and Global Trade:** "Virtual water trade" refers to the hidden flow of water if food or other commodities are traded from one place to another. For example, importing a country's crops also imports its water usage.

26. **Supercooling Water:** Water can be cooled below its freezing point without turning into ice, a state known as supercooled water, often observed in cloud droplets at high altitudes.

27. **The Water Cycle's Age:** The Earth's water cycle is ancient, with water continuously circulating for billions of years, meaning the water you drink today could have once been sipped by a dinosaur.

28. **Water's Sound in Hot vs. Cold:** Hot water and cold water sound different when poured. This is due to the viscosity and surface tension of the water changing with temperature, affecting the size of the bubbles formed.

29. **Fish Drinking Water:** Saltwater fish drink water actively due to osmosis, whereas freshwater fish rarely drink, instead absorbing water through their skin and gills.

30. **The Pressure at Ocean Depths:** At the deepest point of the ocean, the pressure is so intense that it can crush a Styrofoam cup to the size of a thimble

due to the weight of the water above.

31. **Bioluminescent Water:** Certain types of algae and plankton can make the water glow blue at night, a phenomenon known as bioluminescence, caused by a chemical reaction within these organisms.

32. **Water Towers of the World:** Mountains are often referred to as the world's water towers because they provide 60-80% of the planet's freshwater through runoff.

33. **The Speed of Groundwater:** Groundwater can move as slowly as a few centimeters per year, making the replenishment of aquifers a painstakingly slow process.

34. **The First Water Pipes:** The Romans built sophisticated aqueducts and plumbing systems over 2,000 years ago, some of which are still in use today, showcasing early human ingenuity in water management.

35. **Water in Products:** It takes about 22 gallons (about 83 liters) of water to make one pound of plastic, illustrating the hidden water used in manufacturing everyday products.

36. **The Weight of Clouds:** A typical cumulus cloud weighs around 1.1 million pounds (about 500,000 kg), all held aloft by the atmosphere despite the weight of the water droplets it contains.

37. **Frost Flowers:** In polar regions and on thin sea ice, delicate ice structures known as frost flowers can form, creating unique ecosystems that harbor bacteria and chemicals.

38. **Water's Role in Global Warming:** Water vapor is the most abundant greenhouse gas in the atmosphere, playing a significant role in the Earth's energy balance and climate system.

39. **The Rarity of Freshwater:** While 71% of the Earth's surface is covered by water, only 2.5% of it is freshwater, and only a fraction of that is accessible for human use.

40. **Osmoregulation in Aquatic Life:** Aquatic organisms have specialized mechanisms to maintain fluid balance (osmoregulation), allowing them to survive in varying salinities.

41. **The Highest Tides:** The Bay of Fundy in Canada experiences the world's highest tides, with water levels rising up to 53 feet (about 16 meters) due to the unique shape of the bay.

42. **Water's Critical Point:** At a specific temperature and pressure (647 K and 22.064 MPa), water reaches a critical point where it no longer exists as either a liquid or gas but as a supercritical fluid with unique properties.

43. **Iceberg Freshwater:** Icebergs are composed of freshwater, having originated from the accumulation and compaction of snow. This makes them potential sources of drinkable water.

44. **The Color of Water in Lakes:** The color of lakes can vary dramatically due to substances dissolved in the water, with hues ranging from blue to green, or even pink in the case of lakes with high concentrations of certain algae or bacteria.

45. **Water's Polarity:** Water's molecular structure makes it a polar molecule, enabling it to dissolve more substances than any other liquid and earning it the title of "universal solvent."

46. **Capillary Action:** Water can move against gravity in narrow spaces, a phenomenon known as capillary action, which is crucial for the transport of water from roots to leaves in plants.

47. **Thermal Vent Ecosystems:** Deep-sea hydrothermal vents release water heated to over 700°F (about 370°C), supporting unique ecosystems that thrive in the absence of sunlight.

48. **Water's Impact on Civilization:** Access to water has shaped the rise and fall of civilizations throughout history, with societies developing along rivers and coasts to harness water for agriculture, transport, and trade.

49. **Atacama Desert Blooms:** The Atacama Desert, one of the driest places on Earth, can burst into bloom with flowers after rare and sporadic rains, showcasing water's life-giving power.

50. **Water and Human Brain Function:** Adequate hydration is crucial for optimal brain function, with dehydration affecting concentration, memory, and mood.

51. **Water's Sound Speed:** Sound travels about four times faster in water than in air, which is why sounds can be heard over longer distances underwater.

52. **Ancient Water Conservation:** The Nabataeans, an ancient Arab people, were pioneers in water

conservation, building sophisticated systems to collect and store rainwater in the desert over 2,000 years ago.

53. **Water in Combustion Engines:** Water injection, a method of introducing water into the combustion chamber of an engine, can increase efficiency and reduce emissions.

54. **The Reflection of Water:** Water's surface can reflect light in a way that creates a natural mirror, a phenomenon that has inspired countless artists and photographers.

55. **Water's Role in Weight Management:** Drinking water before meals can help promote weight loss by creating a sense of fullness, leading to reduced calorie intake.

56. **The Healing Properties of Water:** Hydrotherapy, the use of water for pain relief and treatment, has been practiced since ancient times, utilizing various temperatures and forms of water.

57. **Water's Freezing Point Depression:** Adding salt to water lowers its freezing point, a principle used in making homemade ice cream and in de-icing roads.

58. **The Water Efficiency of Plants:** Some plants, like cacti and succulents, have adapted to arid environments by developing highly efficient water storage and conservation mechanisms.

59. **Water's Role in Global Trade:** The shipping industry, which relies heavily on waterways, accounts for a significant portion of global trade, highlighting water's importance in the economy.

60. **The Rarity of Drinkable Water in the Universe:** Despite water's abundance in the universe, liquid water suitable for drinking is exceedingly rare, making Earth's water resources uniquely valuable.

61. **The Cultural Significance of Water:** Water holds profound cultural and spiritual significance in many societies, symbolizing purity, life, and renewal.

62. **Water and Global Health:** Access to clean water and sanitation is a key factor in reducing disease transmission and improving public health worldwide.

63. **The Physics of Water Dimples:** The dimple effect, seen when a drop of water falls onto a surface, is caused by the complex interplay of forces, including surface tension and viscosity.

64. **Water's Critical Role in Photosynthesis:** Water is a crucial component in photosynthesis, the process by which plants convert sunlight into energy, releasing oxygen as a byproduct.

65. **The Discovery of Water on Mars:** Evidence of water ice and even seasonal liquid water flows on Mars has significant implications for the possibility of life and future human exploration.

66. **Water's Influence on Climate:** The distribution and movement of water in the atmosphere are major drivers of weather patterns and climate systems.

67. **The Economic Value of Water:** The concept of "blue gold" refers to water's increasing economic value in a world facing water scarcity and competition for resources.

68. **Water in Literature and Mythology:** Water is a

recurring motif in literature and mythology, often representing transformation, danger, or the unconscious mind.

69. **The Water Content of the Human Body:** The human body is composed of up to 60% water, varying with age, gender, and body composition.

70. **Water's Role in Cooking:** Water is essential in cooking, affecting the texture, flavor, and nutritional value of food through processes like boiling, steaming, and simmering.

71. **The Impact of Water Temperature on Fish:** Water temperature significantly affects the metabolism and behavior of fish, influencing their feeding, growth, and reproductive patterns.

72. **Water's Contribution to the Greenhouse Effect:** Water vapor is the most abundant greenhouse gas in the atmosphere, playing a crucial role in regulating the Earth's temperature.

73. **The Use of Water in Power Generation:** Hydropower is one of the oldest and most widely used renewable energy sources, converting the energy of flowing or falling water into electricity.

74. **The Psychological Effects of Water:** Being near water can have calming effects on the mind, reducing stress and promoting mental well-being, a phenomenon sometimes referred to as "blue space."

75. **Water's Role in Geothermal Energy:** Water heated by the Earth's internal heat can be used to generate geothermal energy, a sustainable and clean source of power.

76. **Self-Cleaning Properties of Water:** Moving water in rivers and streams can naturally purify itself through aeration and the action of beneficial bacteria, a process vital for maintaining aquatic ecosystems.

77. **Water's Role in Earth's Interior:** Water exists deep within the Earth's mantle, trapped in minerals, influencing volcanic activity and the movement of tectonic plates.

78. **The Phenomenon of Superheating:** Water can be heated beyond its boiling point without boiling, a dangerous phenomenon known as superheating, often occurring in microwaves.

79. **Water's Contribution to Soil Formation:** Water contributes to the weathering of rock, leading to soil formation, which is essential for plant life and agriculture.

80. **The Influence of Moon on Water:** The Moon's gravitational pull influences the Earth's tides, affecting marine life, coastal ecosystems, and human activities related to the sea.

81. **Water in Firefighting:** Water's high heat capacity makes it effective in absorbing heat, making it a primary tool for firefighting, aside from its ability to smother flames.

82. **The Sound of Boiling Water:** The sound of water beginning to boil is caused by air bubbles forming and collapsing in the water, a precursor to the full rolling boil.

83. **Water's Impact on Light:** Water can bend light, a

phenomenon known as refraction, which is why objects under water appear distorted or closer than they are.

84. **The Scarcity of Blue Lakes:** Truly blue lakes are rare because water is inherently slightly blue, and most lakes reflect the sky or contain sediments and organisms that change their color.

85. **Water's Role in Cement Curing:** Water is crucial in curing cement, a process where water reacts with cement to harden it, highlighting water's role in construction.

86. **The Formation of Hot Springs:** Hot springs are formed when water heated by geothermal energy rises to the surface, creating natural pools of warm to hot water.

87. **Water's Use in Cooling Systems:** Water's thermal properties make it an excellent coolant in industrial processes, power generation, and vehicle radiators.

88. **The Rarity of Pure Water in Nature:** Pure water, $H2O$ without any impurities, is extremely rare in nature due to water's ability to dissolve and carry minerals and gases.

89. **Water's Role in Human History:** Access to water has shaped human settlements, agriculture, and civilizations throughout history, underscoring its strategic importance.

90. **The Concept of Water Stress:** Water stress occurs when the demand for water exceeds the available amount during a certain period or when its quality restricts use.

91. **Water's Influence on Global Security:** Competition over water resources has the potential to lead to conflicts, making water security a critical issue in international relations.

92. **The Discovery of Exoplanets with Water:** Scientists have discovered exoplanets with signs of water vapor in their atmospheres, indicating the potential for life beyond Earth.

93. **The Use of Water in Dyeing Fabric:** Water is essential in the textile industry, particularly in the dyeing process, where it is used to apply color to fabric.

94. **Water's Role in Digestion:** Water is crucial for digestion, helping to break down food, absorb nutrients, and prevent constipation by moving waste through the digestive tract.

95. **The Creation of Snowflakes:** Snowflakes form when water vapor in the air freezes into ice crystals, with each snowflake's unique shape influenced by temperature and humidity.

96. **Water's Effect on Climate Change:** Melting ice and snow due to global warming contribute to rising sea levels, highlighting water's central role in climate change discussions.

97. **The Use of Water in Space Exploration:** Water is not only sought after for sustaining life in space but also considered as a fuel source, with hydrogen and oxygen being key components for rocket fuel.

98. **Water's Historical Use in Timekeeping:** Water clocks, or clepsydras, were among the earliest

timekeeping devices, using the flow of water to measure time.

99. **The Psychological Benefits of Water Sounds:** The sound of running water, such as streams or waves, has been shown to reduce stress and promote relaxation.

100. **Water's Future Challenges:** As the global population grows and climate change intensifies, managing water sustainably, ensuring equitable access, and protecting water ecosystems will be among humanity's most pressing challenges.

Conclusion: The Future of Liquid Gold

Reflecting on the moral and ethical imperatives of managing water sustainably is akin to peering into the very soul of humanity. It's a profound acknowledgment that every drop of water coursing through our rivers, resting in our lakes, or falling from our skies is a testament to life itself. The stewardship of this precious resource is not merely an environmental concern but a profound moral and ethical obligation. It's about recognizing that water, in all its forms, is the common thread weaving through the tapestry of life, connecting us to each other and to the planet in an intricate dance of existence.

Call to Action: A Ripple of Urgency and Compassion

The time to address the water crisis is not tomorrow; it was yesterday. Readers, policymakers, and corporations are called upon to not just witness the unfolding crisis but to become active participants in crafting solutions. It's a call that demands urgency, for the clock ticks loudly against a backdrop of increasing scarcity and pollution. Yet, it's also a call that requires compassion, understanding that the burden of the water crisis often falls heaviest on the shoulders of the most vulnerable among us.

- **Readers** are encouraged to become advocates for water conservation in their communities, to educate themselves and others about the importance of sustainable water practices, and to support policies and initiatives that prioritize the health of our waterways.

- **Policymakers** must rise to the challenge of enacting and enforcing regulations that protect water resources, promote equitable access, and ensure that water management strategies are built on the foundations of sustainability and justice.

- **Corporations** hold a unique power and responsibility to lead by example, to innovate in the realm of water stewardship, and to operate in a manner that respects the finite nature of water and its critical importance to ecosystems and communities alike.

Closing Thoughts: The Interconnectedness of Humanity

- Our shared dependence on water is a poignant reminder of our interconnectedness. Across continents and cultures, water flows as a universal life force, a source of sustenance, culture, and livelihood. The challenges we face in managing water sustainably are not isolated struggles but shared hurdles that call for collective action, empathy, and a renewed commitment to the common good.

Appendix: Water Crisis by the Numbers

The global water crisis is a multifaceted issue, encompassing water scarcity, pollution, and consumption. Here is a statistical overview that sheds light on the magnitude of these challenges:

Global Water Scarcity

- **2.2 billion people** live without access to safe drinking water. (Source: WHO/UNICEF, 2019)

- **4 billion people** experience severe water scarcity for at least one month each year. (Source: Science Advances, 2016)

- By 2025, **two-thirds of the world's population** may face water shortages. (Source: UN-Water)

Water Pollution

- Over **80%** of the world's wastewater is discharged without treatment, contaminating rivers, lakes, and oceans. (Source: UN-Water)

- **Agricultural runoff** is the leading cause of water pollution in rivers and lakes globally. (Source: EPA)

- **Microplastics** have been found in over 80% of tap water samples worldwide, highlighting the pervasive nature of plastic pollution. (Source: Orb Media)

Water Consumption

- Agriculture accounts for approximately **70%** of global freshwater withdrawals, with industry and domestic use accounting for 19% and 11%, respectively. (Source: FAO)

- The average global water footprint—the total volume of fresh water used to produce the goods and services consumed by an individual or community—is **1,385 m³ per year per person**. (Source: Water Footprint Network)

- **Virtual water trade**, the hidden flow of water if food or other commodities are traded from one place to another, significantly impacts water distribution and scarcity. For example, it takes about 15,000 liters (3,963 gallons) of water to produce 1 kg of beef. (Source: Water Footprint Network)

Resources for Further Reading and Involvement

For those looking to deepen their understanding of the water crisis and explore ways to contribute to water conservation efforts, the following resources offer valuable information and avenues for involvement:

United Nations Water (UN-Water)

- **Website:** unwater.org[1]

---

1. https://www.unwater.org

- **Overview:** Coordinates the UN's work on water and sanitation, offering comprehensive reports and data on global water issues.

Water.org

- **Website:** water.org[2]

- **Overview:** Dedicated to providing safe drinking water and sanitation to communities around the world, Water.org offers opportunities for donations and advocacy.

The Water Project

- **Website:** thewaterproject.org[3]

- **Overview:** Focuses on sustainable water projects in sub-Saharan Africa, with options for donations, fundraising, and education on water issues.

World Resources Institute (WRI) - Aqueduct

- **Website:** wri.org/aqueduct

- **Overview:** Provides tools and data for mapping and analyzing water risks around the globe.

Water Footprint Network

---

2. https://www.water.org

3. https://www.thewaterproject.org

- **Website:** waterfootprint.org

- **Overview:** Offers insights into the water footprint concept, including how to calculate and reduce personal and corporate water footprints.

Glossary of Terms: Water Management and Policy

Understanding the terminology used in discussions about water management and policy is crucial for engaging with the global dialogue on water sustainability and conservation. Here's a glossary of key terms and concepts:

Aquifer

- **Definition:** An underground layer of water-bearing rock or materials (gravel, sand, silt, or clay) from which groundwater can be extracted using a water well.

Desalination

- **Definition:** The process of removing salt and other minerals from saline water (like sea or brackish water) to produce fresh water suitable for human consumption or irrigation.

Eutrophication

- **Definition:** A process where water bodies become overly enriched with nutrients (nitrogen and phosphorus), leading to excessive growth of algae and depletion of oxygen in the water, which can cause the death of aquatic life.

Greywater

- **Definition:** Wastewater generated in households or office buildings from streams without fecal contamination, such as sinks, showers, baths, and washing machines, which can be recycled on-site for uses such as landscape irrigation and constructed wetlands.

Integrated Water Resources Management (IWRM)

- **Definition:** A process that promotes the coordinated development and management of water, land, and related resources to maximize economic and social welfare in an equitable manner without compromising the sustainability of vital ecosystems.

Riparian Rights

- **Definition:** The entitlement of a landowner to the natural water flow through or from their property, including the right to use adjacent watercourses and the right to prevent pollution or excessive diversion by upstream neighbors.

Sustainable Water Management

- **Definition:** The management of water resources in a way that meets current human and ecological needs without compromising the ability of future generations to meet their own needs, ensuring a balance between water availability, water quality, and water use.

Virtual Water

- **Definition:** The volume of water used to produce consumer products, including the water used in the production process of agricultural and industrial products. It's a concept used to understand water use in global trade.

Water Footprint

- **Definition:** The total volume of fresh water used to produce the goods and services consumed by an individual or community, or produced by a business. It's a measure of water use that includes both direct and indirect consumption.

Water Scarcity

- **Definition:** A situation that occurs when the demand for water exceeds the available amount during a certain period or when poor quality restricts its use. Water scarcity can result from a combination of low rainfall, high usage, and pollution.

Water Stress

- **Definition:** A condition where the demand for water exceeds the available amount during a certain period, or when its use is restricted by its quality or legal restrictions. It's a more general and less severe condition than water scarcity.

Watershed (or Catchment Area)

- **Definition:** The land area that drains rainwater or snow into one location such as a stream, lake, or wetland. Management of watersheds is crucial for maintaining water quality and supply in a region.

Basin Management: The management of water resources based on the natural boundaries of a watershed or river basin, rather than political or administrative boundaries, to ensure integrated management of surface water and groundwater.

Bioaccumulation: The accumulation of substances, such as pesticides or other chemicals, in an organism. This occurs when an organism absorbs a substance at a rate faster than that at which the substance is lost by catabolism and excretion.

Catchment Area: The area from which rainfall flows into a river, lake, reservoir, or other body of water; also known as a drainage basin or watershed.

Conjunctive Use: The coordinated and integrated management of both surface water and groundwater resources in order to maximize the efficient use of the total water supply in a given area.

Demand Management: Strategies aimed at controlling water demand, including water conservation measures, the use of pricing to encourage water saving, and the promotion of water-efficient technologies.

Ecological Flow (E-flow): The quantity, timing, and quality of freshwater flows and levels necessary to sustain freshwater and estuarine ecosystems and the human livelihoods and well-being that depend on these ecosystems.

Algal Bloom: A rapid increase or accumulation in the population of algae in freshwater or marine water systems, often resulting in a discoloration of the water. While some blooms are harmless, others can produce toxic compounds that pose serious risks to wildlife, pets, and humans.

Aquifer Depletion: The removal of groundwater from an aquifer at a rate faster than it can be naturally replenished, leading to a decline in the water level. This can result in reduced water availability for drinking and agriculture, as well as environmental damage such as land subsidence.

Circular Water Economy: An approach to water management that promotes the reuse and recycling of water within a system, minimizing waste and enhancing the efficiency of water use. This concept aligns with broader principles of circular economy, aiming to create a sustainable, closed-loop system that mimics natural processes.

Drip Irrigation: A highly efficient irrigation method that delivers water directly to the roots of plants through a network of valves, pipes, tubing, and emitters. Drip irrigation minimizes water loss due to evaporation or runoff and is particularly beneficial in arid regions.

Floodplain Management: The operation of a community program of preventive and corrective measures to reduce flood damage, including but not limited to emergency preparedness plans, flood control works, and floodplain management regulations.

Hydraulic Fracturing (Fracking): A method of oil and gas extraction that involves injecting fluid into subterranean rock formations at high pressure to create fractures, allowing oil or gas to flow out to a well. The process uses significant amounts of water and has been associated with groundwater contamination and other environmental concerns.

Non-Revenue Water (NRW): Water that has been produced and is "lost" before it reaches the customer. Losses can be real losses (through leaks, also referred to as physical losses) or apparent losses (through theft or metering inaccuracies). High levels of NRW indicate poor efficiency within a water system.

Permaculture: A system of agricultural and social design principles centered around simulating or directly utilizing the patterns and features observed in natural ecosystems. Permaculture aims to create sustainable ways of living by integrating water-saving practices into food production and community development.

Rain Garden: A planted depression or a hole that allows rainwater runoff from urban areas, like roofs, driveways, walkways, and compacted lawn areas, the opportunity to be absorbed. This reduces rain runoff by allowing stormwater to soak into the ground, as opposed to flowing into storm drains and surface waters which causes erosion, water pollution, flooding, and diminished groundwater.

Stormwater Management: The effort to reduce runoff of rainwater or melted snow into streets, lawns, and other sites and the improvement of water quality, according to the United States Environmental Protection Agency (EPA).

Watershed Management: The study and management of the relevant physical, biological, and human mechanisms and interactions that control water resources and the ecosystem's health within a watershed.

Zero Liquid Discharge (ZLD): A water treatment process designed to remove all the liquid waste from a system. The goal of ZLD is to eliminate liquid waste and maximize water efficiency, making it an ideal solution for industries in water-scarce regions or those looking to reduce their environmental footprint.

Effluent: Treated or untreated wastewater that flows out of a treatment plant, sewer, or industrial outfall. Generally refers to wastes discharged into surface waters.

Groundwater Recharge: The process by which water moves downward from surface water to groundwater. This is a critical process in sustaining aquifer levels and ensuring the availability of groundwater over time.

Potable Water: Water that is safe enough to be consumed by humans or used with low risk of immediate or long-term harm. Also known as drinking water.

Sanitation: The provision of facilities and services for the safe disposal of human urine and feces. Sanitation also refers to the maintenance of hygienic conditions, through services such as garbage collection and wastewater disposal.

Transboundary Waters: Any surface or groundwater system that crosses political boundaries, such as rivers, lakes, or aquifer systems shared by two or more countries.

Water Governance: The political, social, economic, and administrative systems in place that influence water's use and management. Governance determines who gets water, when, and how, and decides who has the right to water and related services.

Water Quality Index (WQI): A numerical indicator that summarizes the overall quality of water in a body of water (like rivers, streams, or lakes) based on various water quality parameters (e.g., pH, dissolved oxygen, turbidity, etc.).

Water Security: The capacity of a population to safeguard sustainable access to adequate quantities of acceptable quality water for sustaining livelihoods, human well-being, and socio-economic development, for ensuring protection against water-borne pollution and water-related disasters, and for preserving ecosystems in a climate of peace and political stability.

Xeriscaping: A landscaping method developed especially for arid and semiarid climates that utilizes water-conserving techniques, such as the use of drought-tolerant plants, mulch, and efficient irrigation.

Did you love *Liquid Gold - The Global Crisis of Water*? Then you should read *Micro Plastic Mega Consequences*[4] by Sophia Fairview!

"Micro Plastic Mega Consequences"

In the pages of "Micro Plastic Mega Consequences," we embark on a journey into the hidden world of microplastics, the tiny invaders with colossal consequences. This meticulously researched and eye-opening book delves into the intricate web of connections between microplastic pollution and the environment, human health, and our rapidly changing climate.

Explore the Unseen Impact:

---

4. https://books2read.com/u/3nG7wP

5. https://books2read.com/u/3nG7wP

Discover how these minuscule particles, often invisible to the naked eye, have infiltrated every corner of our planet, from the deepest ocean trenches to the remotest mountain peaks. "Micro Plastic Mega Consequences" unveils the astonishing ways in which microplastics are shaping our world.

Reveal the Ecological Puzzle:

Unravel the mystery of how microplastics affect marine life, from the tiniest plankton to the mightiest whales. Dive into the intricate food webs where microplastics disrupt the delicate balance of ocean ecosystems, ultimately influencing the food on our plates.

Navigate the Human Connection:

This book goes beyond science to explore the very human dimensions of the microplastic crisis. From seafood contamination to economic impacts on coastal communities and the profound cultural ties to our oceans, "Micro Plastic Mega Consequences" examines the broader implications for societies around the world.

Unlock Climate Dynamics:

Discover how climate change and microplastic pollution engage in complex feedback loops, potentially amplifying each other's impact. Gain insights into the surprising ways in which microplastics interact with climate systems and carbon cycling, influencing our planet's future.

A Call to Action:

As we journey through the pages of "Micro Plastic Mega Consequences," we are confronted with the urgency of addressing this global challenge. This book serves as a rallying cry to protect our oceans, safeguard biodiversity, and combat climate change. It offers a path forward, with practical solutions and a vision for a cleaner, healthier world.

If you are curious about the invisible threat lurking in our environment, if you are concerned about the future of our oceans and planet, and if you are inspired to make a difference, "Micro Plastic Mega Consequences" is a must-read. Join us on this exploration of science, ecology, and human society, and be empowered to take action against the mega consequences of microplastics.

Also by Sophia Fairview

Micro Plastic Mega Consequences
The Dark Side of the Vatican
Saints and Sinners: The Untold Stories of Abuse in the
catholic church
Liquid Gold - The Global Crisis of Water